Whose Side Are You On, Ref?

Whose Side Are You On, Ref?

Norman Burtenshaw
Foreword by Brian Clough

Arthur Barker Limited
London

ISBN 0 213 16437 X

Printed in Great Britain by
Willmer Brothers Limited, Birkenhead

Contents

Illustrations

Foreword

I take no pleasure whatsoever in writing the foreword to this book because its publication marks the end of the career of a referee I believe to be the best this country has produced, certainly in my time in football.

I think it is a nonsense and a tragedy that Norman Burtenshaw should be compulsorily retired at a time when he seems to be at the peak of his powers. He's much fitter now, at forty-seven, than just about any other referee in the game and I consider it is time for the authorities who govern the game to examine their retirement policy.

Would it involve too much work for the League to keep a regular check on refereeing standards, removing those who consistently fell below par, whether they were thirty-seven or forty-seven and retaining those, like Norman Burtenshaw, who maintain a high level of performance, whether they are forty-seven or fifty-seven?

There has never been a referee who did not make mistakes any more than there have ever been players and managers who didn't drop clangers. But Norman Burtenshaw always demonstrated a judgement, dedication and common-sense which made him less prone to error than anyone else.

His views of the shadier practices of soccer run close to my own and I wish him the very best in his reluctant retirement. It's been a pleasure to watch him and he will be missed by everybody who enjoys seeing a man at the peak of his profession.

BRIAN CLOUGH,
Manager, Derby County F.C.
May 1973.

Preface

The Pre-match talk

Why me? Why have I been mixed up in so much controversy in my career as a referee? I am often asked that question. Truthfully I answer that I am never sure. I didn't seek controversy.

I think perhaps I got involved more than most because I never believed in compromises. If the player who scored the only goal of the match was offside I gave it offside even if there were only seconds of the game remaining and I knew the home fans would probably want to tear me to pieces. If I added up a total of six minutes injury time I would play six minutes over. My life has been threatened many times and once I was assaulted by a player. Being a big-match referee doesn't endear you to many people, not even to your family. You are away from home so much they rarely see you. My children were in their teens before I realized it. There is one quality the big-match referee needs above all others: courage. He has to call it the way he sees it.

Sometimes when a particularly difficult match is in the early seconds of injury time, the score is 1–1 and the home side is happy, the away side and the crowd are happy, there is the temptation for the referee to say, 'All right, that's enough, let's call it a day.' But there might still be a minute or two left on his watch that no one knows about. I never made that kind of compromise. I knew that made me disliked. I was never a matey referee with the players as some referees are.

I had a job to do and I knew that whatever decision I made

it would be unpopular with some of the people most of the time. The only way to make sure I had the respect of the majority of top officials and managers was to be as certain as I could that I made the right decision in an honest way. And you can't give the game more than that.

1

Why aren't we loved?

The referee is the man in black out there on the football pitch who is being jeered by the crowd. Most likely the players are abusing him too. No one, it seems, likes a referee. Sometimes we are assaulted, as I was once. Telephone cranks have threatened they would 'do' me. It made a celebrated case.

Only a goal by the home side gives the average football crowd more pleasure than the sight of the ball accidentally striking the referee and knocking him down. I know because it happened to me in 1965 at Easter. The match was Brentford v Southend, a difficult match to control. The ball struck me on the ear and I was knocked out. I was told the crowd reacted with some very amusing comments, such as, 'Don't bring him round, bury the twit.' When I came to, I discovered that my balance was affected. Really I should have gone off and the linesman should have taken over. But it was a hard match and I was unwilling to expose one of my linesmen to its pressures. So I carried on. At the end of the game I was violently sick and was taken to hospital where I had to stay three days. It was my son Paul's eleventh birthday and taking him to Griffin Park had been his birthday treat. Besides the worry of wondering what was wrong with me, I had to stew about how he was going to get home by himself to Bradwell, our home near Great Yarmouth. But Brentford officials were very kind. They took him to Liverpool Street station by car and put him in the care of the Norwich City team who were travelling back to Norfolk after their match.

1

My friends often tell me the kind of things that are said in the stand when football fans open their programme and read who the referee is. 'No, not him again,' is the usual comment. The fans hate us, and so do some managers and players. Malcolm Allison, then Manchester City manager and now manager of Crystal Palace is often saying bad things about referees. He certainly gives me that impression when he comes into the dressing-room with his team sheet before a game. He stares straight through you and says nothing.

Once in a match at Millwall the elastic went in my shorts and I had to send for a new pair and change on the pitch. Under my shorts I wore a swimming costume. There was no indecent exposure! But later some Millwall fans wrote a letter to the FA complaining at my conduct. The letter, I believe, was ignored. It was just another example of the way spectators dislike referees and try and get at them.

Most professionals in the football game look on referees as incompetent amateurs – a necessary evil. They think that because we have not played professional football at the highest level – with two exceptions, Bob Matthewson and Peter Reeves – we are unable to understand the game and its fouls, its pressures and its cheating. In short, they are contemptuous of us.

I played football until I was twenty-five, so I do know something of what it is like to be a player. I was once sent off at the age of twenty-one for using abusive language! I do not claim that my playing experience at this low level qualifies me as an expert about top-class professional football. But I do say that twenty years of refereeing have made me an expert about refereeing. The average time it takes for a referee to get on to the Football League list is about ten years. Do footballers serve an apprenticeship as long as that? Does anyone else in any other job?

Does anyone think that Bobby Moore would make a good referee if he stopped playing tomorrow and became a League referee? He would command the respect of the players until the moment he made his first mistake. Once a referee has lost respect he loses control. And refereeing is about controlling players and seeing that the game is played in the spirit of the laws of the game. You learn about controlling players in the public parks and on the sports grounds. You master things at that level and then you progress to the next level, amateur and semi-professional leagues. Eventually you are ready to face a 60,000 crowd at Old Trafford.

A cricketer can retire, take an examination and emerge the next season as a fully qualified umpire, because cricket umpiring is about making decisions without the hazard of gesticulating players and intimidation. A cricket umpire is allowed to make his decisions without these kinds of pressures. Cricketers do not attack the umpire physically, as happened to me in Belgium.

The pressure in football comes from having to control highly emotional, excitable people. Making the decision is the easy part. What comes next – implementing it – is the hard bit, which is why the apprenticeship of the referee is long and arduous. Only the tough referees with the strong personalities survive and get to the top. There are 85 referees on the Football League list, 23 supplementary referees, 281 linesmen and 82 assessors. I cannot think of one referee who has a weak personality. It is said that ex-players would make better referees because they would spot the so-called professional fouls quicker than the 'amateur' referee. They would pick up the foul which the players condemn most of all, the 'over-the-top' tackle. This is when one player's foot goes over the ball and catches the other player on the leg.

A good example of this kind of tackle came in the Crystal Palace v Leeds match in the 1972–3 season. Norman Hunter, the Leeds centre-back, committed it on John Craven, the Crystal Palace centre-forward. The match was televised by ITV and millions of people saw it. So did the referee, Bob Matthewson. You may think that Matthewson, one of the few ex-players to become a top-class referee, should have sent Hunter off the field, because he, more than most referees, would know the gravity of Hunter's offence. But Hunter stayed on the field. Matthewson may have been right. I do not know. I make this point merely to demonstrate that ex-players who become referees may not necessarily respond the way it is said they will.

Most times when a referee signals the end of a match and he leaves the field with his linesmen, ball in hand, he is at the least booed and may have to be surrounded by police. On occasions, missiles are thrown. At Queens Park Rangers I was once struck by a toilet-roll, which is nothing; some referees have been felled by coins, bottles and cans, but fortunately that has not happened to me. I am never worried or frightened about leaving the field. For the supporters to boo is a natural reaction. They pay their 40p admission and are entitled to boo what they like or who they like and a referee has to be immune to it. I find that the home crowd tends to boo the referee if their team is not playing well. It follows a pattern: first they blame the referee; his decisions are preventing their team from winning; they resent this; later they realize that perhaps it is not the referee's fault after all; perhaps their own players are to blame and they start barracking the home team, chanting for the substitute to come on or abusing the manager; at the end of the game, however, the final boos are reserved for the referee.

I say to players that I never make a mistake. They think I am joking, but if they look at the laws of the game they will see that the decision of the referee is final. This means I cannot make a mistake because my opinion is the one that counts. If I decide that Geoff Hurst has handled intentionally, then Geoff Hurst has handled intentionally. The TV cameras may prove otherwise, but during the game my decision is the vital one.

The referee does not give a decision for the home team, the away team or anyone else, but because he thinks he is right. He gives that decision honestly. The integrity of the referee in this country is beyond dispute. There has never been a bent referee in the history of the Football League. But some players have been convicted of selling a match.

Of course, no referee is perfect. Jeff Blockley handled on the goal line in a match between Arsenal and Manchester City in the 1972–3 season and everyone at Highbury seemed to see it except referee Gordon Hill and his linesmen. The ball would have gone into the net but Blockley, the Arsenal centre-half, punched it away. Gordon Hill, one of our top referees, said he failed to see the incident because of the sun in his eyes. The linesman on that side of the field said his view was blocked. Mr Hill gave his decision – no penalty. He was right; he saw no hand-ball offence so how could he give a penalty? That would have been dishonest. It was unfortunate but this incident was counterbalanced by another when Manchester City were

4

awarded a goal at White Hart Lane when Lee admitted punching the ball in. I was the unfortunate referee. Like Gordon Hill, I didn't see it.

If we are reviled so much, why do we do it? I can only speak of myself. I love football and being involved in football. The high point of my existence is Saturday afternoon; there is nothing more exhilarating than stepping out at Old Trafford or Anfield or Highbury in front of a packed crowd.

It is not a question of ego, of liking to be seen by so many people and having power over the emotions they are about to generate. I do not look on myself as a vain person. Eleven years of refereeing in the Football League have not altered my personality or my nature – at least, I do not think they have!

I try not to look at the crowd. I do not want to be involved. I want to be in a world of my own where I can concentrate. I like to think I am in the same tense state as the players. I am tense because I want to do well. If I am relaxed there is more likelihood that I will miss something. If I find I am tending to let other things come into my thoughts, I tell myself: 'Come on, Norman. Get hold of this game.'

I am forty-seven, happily married with a daughter of twenty-three and a son of nineteen who plays football and was once sent off for allegedly striking a player. I live in a bungalow at Bradwell, a small village in Norfolk. It cost £2,500 nine years ago.

When I started refereeing I worked as a night telephone operator. Some days I would work all night and travel next day straight to a match. It was difficult to get time off so I resigned and bought a sweet-shop one hundred yards from my house. The turnover is not large and I am still paying off the mortgage.

The money I make from football is useful. But it is not the reason why I am in football. No referee is in it for the money. We were paid £10.50 a match (the fee has now been raised) plus £6 overnight allowance, £4 meal allowance, and 3p a mile for using our car or first-class train fare if we go by train. Three pence a mile is less than the AA estimate for running a car; the Football League prefer you to travel by rail. Living in Norfolk as I do, I often have to take the car. I have a Volkswagen and a radio is essential. I would go bonkers sometimes, driving hundreds of miles on a Friday and Saturday without one.

Would I be a better referee if I were paid £100 a match? I do not think so. I do it because I like doing it and it keeps me in football.

Many referees are self-employed like me because it is difficult to get time off in a normal five-day-a-week job. Some of them own their businesses. The majority have one thing in common: they have jobs where they are in charge of other people.

Referees are aged between thirty-five and forty-seven. Forty-seven is the retiring age. You may feel superbly fit and run ten miles a day but when your forty-seventh birthday comes, that is it. No one is reprieved. However, on the Continent there are some referees who continue until they are past fifty. I should have liked to continue past fifty myself. I am fit enough to do so, but the League ruling says you must go at forty-seven, and I went.

What do referees do when they retire? Some just fade away but others become assessors. These are the people who go to matches and report on referees. They fill in a big form saying whether the referee was in control of the game as he should have been. They comment on his application of the laws, his positioning and fitness, his signals, his co-operation with linesmen and the way he applied the advantage. ('Advantage' is letting the game continue when one side has broken one of the laws. To stop the game would penalize the innocent team which has possession of the ball. Hence the phrase 'giving the advantage'). The Football League brought in the assessor system in season 1970-1 in an effort to improve the standard of refereeing which was then, as now, under continual attack from inside and outside the game.

One assessor wrote criticizing my arm action when making a decision. He said: 'This unnecessary flailing signal means nothing but suggests annoyance at someone having the audacity to commit an offence.' The assessor was right. Perhaps this mannerism did offend. But in my mind at the time were two thoughts – not to allow myself to get involved in an argument with a player, and to get the game started again as soon as possible.

6

I do not believe in talking to players unless I have to. I wave them away. If I get into a conversation I may miss something behind me. No good has ever come of discussing a decision with a player once it is made. There is nothing more time-wasting and frustrating.

After one West Ham match at Upton Park on 3 April 1971 an assessor wrote: 'At the end of the game you gesticulated by punching the sky, probably in delight. This could convey to players and spectators that you were involved emotionally in the match as much as they were. If there is a tendency towards this, the best advice would be for you to try and resist it.' What the assessor could not have known was that the match was my last before refereeing the FA Cup Final at Wembley and I was expressing my delight at having come through the game without injury! But I do get involved, there is no denying it.

The assessors allot markings out of ten for each match. These are sent to the Football League headquarters at Lytham St Annes. The home and away clubs also give marks up to ten, so there are three different people marking the referee. If you disallow a goal some managers are resentful and give you low marks, but the general rule is that the club marks are nearly always the same as the assessor's verdict.

These marks are recorded and at the end of the season the referees near the top of the table receive a £50 bonus, the referee in the middle £37.50 bonus and those at the bottom £25. The amounts have now been increased, but the marks are secret. You only know which group you are in according to how much you receive.

Some footballers receive £50 a match as a bonus. Referees have to do well to earn that in a season! Assessors are volunteers and receive only their expenses. If a referee's marks are low he is told about it, but hardly any referees are sacked after only one season on the League list.

Experience and the application of common sense in the face of considerable mental pressures are the qualities which contribute most to a referee's success, and no one gets experience if he is sacked in his first season. Two or three seasons usually elapse before a decision is made about sacking anyone. You have to be pretty good to get as far as the League list, so it is unlikely that a referee will be disposed of so quickly once he makes the list.

There are different types of referees and few use the same methods. John Homewood, the FIFA referee from Sunbury-on-Thames, is a shouter. He shouts a lot on the field at the players. Someone once said to him that having reached the international list he should start quietening down. He replied that he got that far by shouting and he intended to carry on that way.

Roger Kirkpatrick of Leicester is something of a showman. He likes miming fouls, and when he runs upfield the crowd invariably cheer him as his legs pump up and down. His antics are not important. The important thing is, does he have control? And he always does because he is a good referee. Why shouldn't the referee be seen to explain his decision to the crowd, if somewhat flamboyantly? He is probably the most needed person on the field. No game could start without him.

Maurice Fussey used to amuse the crowd with his fast sprints. Ken Dagnall of Bolton was a slow mover, but was always on the fringe of an incident, and was one of the finest referees produced in England. I am a physical referee myself.

Roy Bailey, the former Ipswich and Crystal Palace goal-keeper, once said I buzzed around the pitch like a bluebottle. You cannot take away a referee's personality. I train hard – several sessions a week on the beach which amount to the same time as the professional footballer trains each week – and I believe in trying to keep up with the play. Brian Clough, the Derby County manager, said at Upton Park in 1972: 'That fellow was so close to the play that he tackled our centre-half twice.'

One referee who shows his enjoyment of his job is Tommy Dawes of Ipswich, known as 'Smiler' Dawes. I am not like that. I do not laugh much and I concentrate so hard that people say I look fierce.

Once I was refereeing a Manchester United match and dis-allowed one of their 'goals'. Maurice Setters was particularly upset about this. Shortly afterwards United scored a legitimate goal.

'That's mucked up your football coupon,' he said. That was one of the few occasions I had a good laugh. Another time was at a Chelsea match when a long ball was played out of defence.

8

It is impossible to keep up with play in those circumstances even if you anticipate what is going to happen. Peter Osgood the Chelsea centre-forward said, 'Why don't you keep up with the play then?'

The only time I tried to say something funny in one of the pre-match talks referees used to have with the players in their dressing-rooms it fell flat. It was a West Ham match. The week before, West Ham had been refereed by Ricky Nicholson whose wig had blown off during the game. When I came in I pointed to my hair and said to the West Ham players, 'I should like to point out that all this is my own.' There was complete silence. I looked round. No one said a word, not even the manager, Ron Greenwood. That showed the tension. A dressing-room is not a happy place before a big match. Intruders are resented, which is one of the reasons why the Football League dropped the idea of ordering referees to give pre-match talks.

Brian Clough was particularly short. 'You'll not have any trouble from these lads,' he said. I have a superstition of always wearing new laces in my boots at every match. I always ask the home club for a pair. One day at the Baseball Ground I knocked on the Derby dressing-room door.

'What the hell do you want?' asked Clough.

'A pair of laces,' I said.

'Give the bugger a pair of white laces,' ordered Clough.

'Sorry,' I said. 'But it will have to be black ones.'

'All right,' said Clough. 'Give the bugger a black pair and for Christ's sake get him out of here.'

I thanked him and left. I knew Clough was not being rude. Men act in odd ways when they are under acute mental stress. Some managers look nervous wrecks before a game. Tony Waddington of Stoke is one of the worst.

One day I was at Tottenham when Bill Nicholson brought in the team sheet. In the past few years League clubs have had to declare their teams to the referee thirty minutes before the kick-off. This regulation came in after several clubs made late changes which angered supporters because they were not told about them. I looked at Nicholson's yellow slip with the eleven names, nominated substitute and the colours. Martin Chivers's name was not on it. After Nicholson left I said to my lines-men, 'Chivers is out then.' We agreed that was peculiar.

9

Chivers, in my view – and I admit I am no expert about judging players other than by their conduct – is a great player. He had made a poor start to the season, but even so it was surprising that he was left out.

When the bell went and the teams came out I saw Nicholson again. Just behind him, stripped and ready, was Chivers. 'I thought Chivers wasn't playing,' I said.

I have rarely seen anyone react in such a startled manner. 'What do you mean?' said Nicholson. 'Of course he's playing.'

'But he's not down on your team sheet,' I said. Nicholson looked aghast. Technically Chivers should not have been playing as he was left out of the official team sheet.

'What are we going to do?' asked Nicholson in a panic.

'You tell me who isn't playing out of this lot and I'll make the alteration,' I said. I told Bob Stokoe, Blackpool's manager, and he accepted it as a genuine error.

It was the common-sense solution, or so I thought. But later when I mentioned it to George Readle, the Football League official responsible for referees at that time, he said I should have reported the incident. I suppose he was right. Nicholson may look composed when he is watching a game but beforehand he is extremely nervous.

Referees are under almost as much pressure and matters have worsened in recent seasons. The Football League make referees responsible for seeing there is no colour clash but while they lay down that there must be colour differences in shirts and socks, nothing is said about shorts. That should be changed because teams playing in light shirts and dark shorts can be confused on black-and-white TV, as has happened when Spurs use their second strip of yellow at Derby, who also wear dark shorts.

At the Leeds v Birmingham City First Division match in 1972–3 Don Revie, the Leeds manager, came to my room before the kick-off and said, 'Isn't there a colour clash? They're in blue and white.'

Leeds were all white. I looked at Birmingham's colours and saw the shirts were royal blue with a white stripe on the front. As there was only one white stripe I decided there was no clash. But both teams wore white shorts.

After the Football League dispensed with pre-match talks,

came the inspection of the studs. The new nylon studs – which I have always thought to be dangerous – were being roughed up on the concrete exits from the dressing-rooms to the tunnel, and in some cases players were receiving gashes down the leg from the tackles of players wearing these studs. Quite rightly the Football League wanted to stop this, so they instructed linesmen to inspect studs before the kick-off. It became quite a controversial issue because the linesmen were supposed to wait in the dressing-rooms after the inspections, and managers claimed that it was a reflection on the integrity of the players.

'Are they going to change their boots when the linesman has gone, in order to maim the opposition?' said the managers.

Nearly all the trouble here would be eliminated if clubs were asked to put down rubber or coconut mats from the dressing-room doors to the edge of the pitch. If the studs made no contact with concrete or macadam they would stay rounded and not be roughed up.

I bring two pairs of boots to each match in case the conditions change. I also have some spare studs. Footballers change their boots and their studs according to the state of the playing surface, so why shouldn't referees? This is one department where referees lack professionalism: some of them wear rubber-studded boots, and as anyone who has ever worn rubbers knows it is impossible to keep one's feet when it is wet.

It is a lonely life being a referee. I always travel the night before unless it is a local match. Living in East Anglia, there is hardly such a thing as a local match! Only rarely did I referee at Ipswich and Colchester. The journey on the Friday night is always a solitary one. You check in at the hotel and spend the evening alone. Next morning I aim to arrive before the laid-down time of one o'clock, or two hours before the kick-off. You inspect the ground and walk round.

From that moment, the tension builds up. A few fans are dribbling in through the turnstiles. Downstairs in the referee's room I am greeting my linesmen. I may not have seen them for years. In season 1973-4 however, the League have tried out a system of teams of a referee and two linesmen staying together.

We discuss old matches and incidents. The referee's room at clubs like Arsenal, Coventry, Tottenham Hotspur and Manchester United is ample in size and well equipped. Highbury officials circulated every referee on the League list and asked each whether he would prefer a bath or a shower. The reply must have been fifty-fifty because now the Highbury referee's room has both. Many clubs do not have a bath, however. I prefer a bath because you can lie in it and relax the muscles. A shower does not allow this. At some clubs the facilities for the officials are deplorable. You begin to accept that there are people in professional football who think the referee is from a lower breed. The referee is often not given the facilities his status deserves.

After the match drinks – tea, beer or a short drink – are sent in. We have our shower or bath, dress, stuff our wet towel in with our kit in the bag and leave quietly. That wet towel rankles. Why should we be expected to bring our own towels? Why can't the club supply them? Yet sometimes when we ask for towels the response is one of incredulity, as though officials suspect our motives.

Referees are not encouraged to go into any of the guest rooms and socialize as cricket umpires socialize after matches. We do not meet the players or the managers afterwards. There have been occasions, although it has never happened to me, when managers have stormed into a referee's room and demanded an explanation of a certain decision. Some referees overlook this, but they are supposed to report the incident. There are some managers who are gentlemen. Bertie Mee of Arsenal is one. Several times he has knocked at my door, poked his head in and said, 'Excellent game, well done.'

As we leave, trying to look anonymous but failing because our bags give us away, reporters in the hallway sometimes try and ask questions. We have to be polite and do our best not to answer them. The Football League frowns on referees making comments about controversial incidents to the Press, though their disapproval has been relaxed recently to permit referees to confirm the names of players cautioned.

There will usually be some fans still outside the ground, waiting for autographs. Not ours though! If the result has gone against their team and they think the referee was to blame, they will shout abuse.

Travelling home by car is always preferable because you are alone, with no one to criticize or to jeer. You play the game through in your mind again. If you travel by train there is the risk that you may encounter hostile supporters. Once, while changing trains at Moorgate after refereeing a match at Highbury, a man ran up behind me and whacked me on the back and ran off. He didn't say anything.

Sometimes a train journey becomes unbearable if fans have taken a dislike to you after recognizing you. This has happened to me. But I have also had many enjoyable trips with fans who just wanted to sit and talk sensibly about the game. Not all of them understand the laws of the game, so when you tell them why you made the decisions you did, they have different views. They are not alone in this. Many players, even internationals of many years' standing, do not know the laws of the game.

In one First Division match two players, both internationals, shouted to a colleague at a goal kick, 'Come up, you're offside.'

I told them, 'You can't be offside at a goal kick.' They did not know that. That kind of conversation takes place every Saturday during the soccer season.

In the Crystal Palace v Everton First Division match in 1972–3 I sent Mel Blyth (Crystal Palace) off for elbowing Alan Whittle (Everton) in the face as they walked back inside the penalty area for a free kick. The ball was dead as I had already blown for a free kick. Yet when Whittle was felled the Everton captain Howard Kendall said to me, 'What about a penalty?' I had to tell him that the ball was dead.

On the other hand there are players who do know the laws of the game perfectly well. There are hundreds who have passed a test on the laws of the game as part of their FA Coaching Certificate.

Late on Saturday night, or sometimes early on Sunday morning, I arrive home. I have been away on average forty-eight hours and earned £10.50 less tax. If I have had a good game I am happy. If I have had a bad game, then it is something to worry about over the weekend. I am back at work on Monday, which is what makes me glad I am not in the game full-time. There is a relief from the pressures. I can cut myself off and go back fresh to the next match.

If I am home early enough I can see football on television. To a young referee it can be distracting to know that the TV cameras are recording his moves and dissecting his decisions.

The referee has to act instantly. There is no play-back for him. He has made his decision and it is the right decision because he made it. The result of the match cannot be changed afterwards because the camera showed that the ball seemed to be out of play before the winger crossed it.

Television never worries me. I treat it like the crowd. I forget it is there when I am at a match. I shut it out of my mind. But I enjoy watching it when I get home. I study the referee and his positioning, the way he handles the players, whether he is in control.

The 1971 Football League memorandum to referees said: 'The League's main interest is that the referees should control the players. How they do this is their own concern as long as do it.' That is what refereeing is all about really – controlling workers in an industry which works in a highly-charged, emotional atmosphere, and seeing that they do not kick lumps out of each other. It is a professional job and I like to think that most of us do it professionally.

2

The game – then and now

When I started refereeing on the League list in 1962-3 the talk
was about defensive football and how it was ruining the game.
My first First Division match was Leicester v Burnley at Filbert
Street. It was a 3-3 draw and I remember coming off thinking
what a wonderful match it had been.

Eleven years later, in my last season on the League list, not
one team in the fourth round of the FA Cup succeeded in scoring three goals until Derby scored five in a replay at White Hart
Lane. The talk was still about defensive football! But now the
talk was justified. Football had become more defensive. The
play was tighter, and I was sure that many of the incidents I
had to deal with were caused by the frustration of players who
wanted to play but couldn't because there was no room on the
pitch. Twenty of the twenty-two players were encompassed in
a twenty-five yard strip of territory. Even Sir Stanley Matthews
and Tom Finney would have found difficulty in operating in
such conditions. These tactics were not used much in 1962-3. I
recall the amount of running I had to do in that Leicester v
Burnley match. The play was so open that I covered every
square foot of the Filbert Street pitch.

Another match I remember that season was Tottenham
Hotspur v Manchester United at White Hart Lane. Spurs won
6-2. I will repeat that. Six goals to two! What a match
that was! Spurs had possibly their greatest side – Danny
Blanchflower, Dave Mackay, Maurice Norman (like me, a
Norfolk man), John White, Cliff Jones and Bobby Smith.

15

Manchester United were one of the finest club sides in the world. Denis Law was in his prime – I marvelled at his skills – Bobby Charlton was playing, and there were names like Pat Crerand, Nobby Stiles, Johnny Giles and Maurice Setters in their side.

The match was played on the day that the Russian ships were steaming towards Cuba in the Cuban missile crisis. All round the ground the cramped supporters were listening to their transistors for the latest news. As far as we knew, this could have been the last football match we should ever see. It would have been a good one to go out on.

The Tottenham players moved the ball around superbly. There always seemed a number of alternatives for the man in possession. Despite the presence of players like Mackay and Smith, Spurs were not a difficult side for a referee to control.

Mackay's tackles were sometimes over-zealous but he didn't argue the way his successors were to argue eleven years later. One gesture or look from Mackay was enough! Blanchflower had the reputation of being a talkative player on the field but he never said much to me.

Bobby Smith was about the only Spurs player who caused me any problems. He gave the impression that he was so keen to score goals that he would put man and ball into the net. He certainly did the unorthodox thing.

Unlike the teams of the seventies, Spurs never brought all their players back when they were under pressure. They left the defenders to defend and the attackers to attack. This made the play freer. Eleven years later, teams had so many players behind the ball that the edge of the penalty area looked like a Paris traffic jam – all clogged up.

Spurs had wingers playing wide in Terry Medwin and Cliff Jones. Medwin was a good crosser of the ball. Jones, so exciting to watch in the dribble, was a brave finisher. Spurs scored 111 goals in their forty-two League matches that season. No club got anywhere near that in my last season.

Yet Spurs did not win the League title. Everton just beat them to it. These were the two richest clubs of the day. They bought most of their stars and were looked on as millionaire clubs.

Manchester United were the glamour side, however, always

16

attracting the biggest attendances away from home. They had a reputation for playing good football but they had some hard players in their ranks. Stiles was always difficult for any referee and Crerand could be fiery. Mark Pearson was often naughty as well. But the player who worried me most was Maurice Setters. Although a good-humoured fellow, he really went in hard.

In those days the managers did not have to submit their team sheets, so the referee had no contact with club officials. I never met Matt Busby; in fact, it was rare to meet anyone. Crowds were generally well behaved. The toilet-roll epidemic had only just started and the chanting of obscenities was yet to come; so was the invasion of pitches by the fans.

There seemed to be more ball players in those days. George Eastham always gave pleasure for Arsenal at Highbury. And I used to enjoy listening to Johnny 'Budgie' Byrne at West Ham. He was one of the game's leading chatterboxes. It was all humorous; never any malice.

Johnny Haynes was in his prime at Fulham. He talked a lot too but his chatter was less pleasant. He could be withering, particularly with some of the comments he made to his colleagues. He caused more rows than any player I knew. But he was a very great player; one of the finest passers in the history of the game. Ten years later I refereed him again in South Africa. He was slower but much of the old skill was still there. And he was still moaning!

UEFA, the European Football Association, issued a directive in season 1962–3 appealing for more sportsmanship. They asked players to shake hands at the end of the game. If a player knocked another over, he ought to help him up and apologize. The directive also called for three cheers for the winners at the end! I never remembered many players arguing with my decisions in those days. They did not go so far as to give three cheers, but decisions were received in a much less emotional way than they were eleven years later. I can never recall being surrounded by a mob of players as I was at Elland Road in 1971 when I allowed the Jack Charlton goal.

Those first few years of my career were perhaps the most enjoyable I had. That first season was the winter of the big snow. There was a total of 261 postponements in the FA Cup. Referees were fed up with inspecting snow-covered pitches and

17

declaring matches off. It was the first year of the pools panel. One of the controversies was about the white ball. Quite rightly, a number of people thought the League should allow the use of orange, yellow or red balls in the snow instead of the customary white ball.

I think I agreed with Sir Alf Ramsey when he wrote in the *FA News* early in 1973 that the present-day footballer was fitter and more skilled in a team sense than his predecessors. In my last season the players were faster and physically better able to sustain a high pace for ninety minutes. The man in possession always found a defender in front of him. Behind that man was another player covering. Stan Matthews never had to withstand this pressure.

Because the players were able to cover more ground there was less space to find, so passes grew shorter in length and the game constricted. Forwards would chase back and tackle. Defenders would forage forward and overlap. The game became jumbled up. Defenders were attacking. Attackers were defending.

It appeared to me that there was too much emphasis in coaching the defensive side of football. Possibly this was because it is easier to organize a defence than an attack. Defenders can follow set tactics. But to succeed in attack, players need to improvise and beat opponents by the unexpected.

The coaches came from the same university, the FA Coaching Scheme, and were taught by the same people. Many of them had similar ideas, so on the field teams cancelled each other out. In short, the game became less entertaining. As the game became tighter the frustrations increased. The player who continually found himself baulked lashed out in anger. Another name went into the book.

Goalscorers exist by scoring goals. If everyone conspires to stop them, they derive less enjoyment from playing. Instead of having half-a-dozen or more chances a game, centre-forwards found themselves down to one or two. The pressure on them was greater.

In my last season it was noticeable that there was more coaching going on in matches. More players were telling other players what to do. They played the game for them. A lot of teams seemed to be following the same pattern of play.

18

Having a good leader on the field was a benefit. Mike Bailey, the Wolverhampton Wanderers captain, was outstanding in this respect. As an exhorter of his fellow players, I would rank him higher than anyone else. But if the play was so predictable that players could direct it with their mouths, then the other side heard the instructions too and another stage was reached in the cancelling-out process.

After the referees' clean-up began in 1971, the game slowly began to improve. Those players who could take the ball past defenders now had a chance to do so without being kicked.

But the win-at-almost-any-cost attitude still prevailed. The scramble to get into the top half-dozen positions in the Football League developed apace. Players showed less and less respect for referees. Not many of them would accept a decision and walk away the way Bobby Moore walks away. They would argue about it. Linesmen would find themselves being abused. If the defending side thought a goal was offside a posse would rush over to the linesman and upbraid him. This never happened in my first season.

These were merely signs of the stress that was being inflicted on the players by the system that demands success. Players had to win to get the big money. It was no use earning £40 in a small club and being happy. You would never save enough to live on after football finished with you. Football was a hard life. I knew two youngsters from my own village who served an apprenticeship with League clubs only to be told they were not good enough to make the grade. They came back home unequipped for a normal job and it was late in the day to begin another apprenticeship.

In my first season there was more laughter in football. There seemed to be more characters. The new breed of player is more dedicated. He gives the appearance of trying harder.

If Charlie George had played in 1962–3 he would have been looked on as an absurdity, with his volatile temperament, long hair and V-signs. Charlie has usually behaved himself when I have had him on the field but some of his exploits – like when he seized a Newcastle player by the throat – have become infamous. By my last season he was still not a great player because to my mind a great player can control himself. Bobby Charlton was the classic example. But Charlie George was popular with many young fans because he represented the way they felt about things. He was a bit of a rebel, standing out against authority, and a lot of young people thought that way too.

I never judged any person by his appearance. Long hair didn't mean that he was a no-good. I like long hair. If it suited me I would have had my hair long myself. But long hair has not been encouraged among referees – it might get in your eyes. One senior referee, Harry New, was told by an assessor to have his hair cut because it was too long. One day a referee will control a League match with a headband keeping his hair in place. It may take some years yet though!

Many of the modern players are a credit to the game, players like Kevin Keegan, Steve Heighway, Chris Lawler and Ray Clemence of Liverpool, John Richards of Wolverhampton, Steve Perryman of Tottenham and Brian Clough's exciting centre-forward Roger Davies. I wish they could have taken part in some of the matches I refereed earlier in my career.

Is there a quick answer to the problem of football becoming tighter and less enjoyable to watch? I do not approve of tinkering with the laws but some serious consideration must be given to changing the offside law. It has been changed before to suit changing conditions and it can be changed again.

I remember taking the Colchester v Luton Watney Cup match when the Watney Cup rules allowed for no offsides outside the penalty area. Colchester took advantage of the experimental rule but Luton didn't. I felt the experiment was not given a long enough trial. Not enough evidence was accumulated. Many people in the game were opposed to it and were not prepared to let it work. But it certainly opened up the midfield. The play was more end to end. The linesmen did not have to hare up and down the line as they do now. They could station themselves on the edge of the 18-yard line to watch for offside. I do not say the Watney Cup idea is the answer. But something like that will have to be tried if the trend in closing up the game continues.

In 1962 defenders did not close up the way they do in 1973. The play was generally between the two penalty areas. In 1973 the playing area was reduced to a twenty-five or thirty-yard strip up and down the field. There would be constant interruptions for offside decisions; crowds became irritated; fans started to stay at home. And the game's rulers began to worry, though not enough to make the necessary changes.

3

The gamesmen

In the old days managers used to shout at players. Players used to shout at referees. Now players are shouting at players: 'You're a so-and-so cheat.' 'Get up, you're not hurt.' 'Do that again and I'll smash your face in.'

This is a sign of the sickness that has crept into the game in recent years. It stems from the introduction of gamesmanship – an all-out effort to make certain the result goes your way without appearing to break the laws. Some people call it professionalism.

Often the crowd has little idea of what is going on because most of it is verbal. A player goes down from a tackle and lies on the ground holding his leg. The player who tackled him shouts, 'I didn't hurt you. You'll get me booked.' The referee is the arbiter. He has to decide whether the man on the ground is acting; whether the player who made the tackle is only saying that because he knew it was a bad one and wants to influence the referee?

This is one of the reasons why I try to be as close to the play as possible. If you are a long way away you can miss the intent. The expression on a player's face can tell much of the story.

One of the first players to be cautioned for pretending to be injured when he wasn't was the Birmingham City forward Trevor Francis. He was the first one I booked for the offence.

The match was Sheffield United v Birmingham City in February 1973. It was a pretty vital First Division relegation game. There had been one or two incidents and I sent Bob

Hatton of Birmingham off for striking an opponent while on the ground. I was bending over them trying to break it up and his right-hander nearly hit me!

Later, I saw Francis suddenly fall down. The nearest Sheffield player said, 'I never touched him, ref.' I told him I could see that. I went to Francis and said, 'I am booking you for feigning injury. You could have got that other player sent off if I hadn't been looking.' Francis – who had a brilliant game, incidentally – said he didn't agree. I said, 'Well, are you injured? Do you want the trainer?' He replied that he didn't want the trainer.

This incensed me. I found it hard to believe that a professional footballer would try to get a colleague sent off the field by such a deceitful trick. When I left Bramall Lane later that evening I was expecting to be asked by the Press whether Francis had been booked. Unfortunately no one asked me; I hoped that some publicity about an aspect of the game the public knew very little about might contribute towards getting the practice of feigning injury stopped. Francis never appealed against his caution.

The player who feigns injury causes a big problem for the referee. According to the laws, the trainer can only be allowed on to treat a player if the player is too bad to walk to the touch-line to be treated. We are much too lenient in this country. On the Continent referees let the play continue and the man who is only slightly hurt knows he has to go off if he wants attention. Here we let the trainer on almost every time a player goes down.

This has led to abuses. A new tactic used by some managers when their side is under heavy pressure is to tell different players to collapse and call for the trainer. The game is stopped and on comes the trainer. No sooner has that player been sprayed or sponged and the game restarted than another player goes down in another part of the field. Again play is stopped. The crowd goes silent. If this happens three or four times in a short space of time the attacking team loses its rhythm. The play-actors have won.

It is easy to say that referees should be more ruthless. But what if one of the players is genuinely injured in a serious manner? What if the referee in the Arsenal v Norwich League Cup tie in 1972 had refused to let the Norwich skipper Duncan

Forbes be treated when, unknown to everyone at Highbury that night including Forbes himself, the player was suffering from a collapsed lung?

What if a player had a broken leg and the referee said, 'Get up, you're acting'? It is not easy!

Harry Medhurst, the Chelsea trainer, once told a meeting of referees that one way of telling if a player was really injured was the way he went down. If he went straight down and stayed down then he was hurt. But if he rolled over and over then he was putting it on.

Two players who have sometimes caused me problems over their injuries are Billy Bremner, the Leeds captain, and Allan Clarke, the Leeds and England striker. In the 1972–3 season, TV-viewers had an opportunity of seeing Bremner twice in eight days during the series of matches between Leeds and Norwich. In the first match Bremner tackled Max Briggs from behind and was quite properly booked. Bremner rose holding his head as though he had been the victim of the tackle.

A week later he tackled Doug Livermore and was again booked. Once more Bremner seemed to be the player who was on the receiving end. He held his thigh and had to be treated by Les Cocker, the Leeds trainer.

Leeds are constantly at the referee, appealing for decisions, complaining about other players and, in some cases, telling the referee to get his book out and caution an opponent. Clarke seems to specialize in this. I do not know why they do it. They are such a great side. They give the appearance of being too clever by half. It begins to wear the referee down. You wonder whether you are right or wrong. The other team say, 'They are conning you, ref.'

Leeds were less disposed to try it when I was refereeing their matches because they knew I would tell them to shut up. They knew they wouldn't get very far. At the start of the 1972–3 season Leeds wanted to give Bremner an armband to distinguish him as the club captain and allow him to speak to the referee. This was hailed as a good idea by some people.

I did not think so. By giving him an armband you were giving him the right to talk to the referee and query his decision. No player should be licensed to dissent. If a player comes up to me with a civil question I will answer it, although

I do not make a habit of speaking to players unless I have to. But if a player comes up shouting I will say, 'Look, I don't shout at you. Don't shout at me.'

Manchester City were a team I never liked having. They had the unenviable reputation of being the mouthiest team in the Football League. I think the players took it from their manager, Malcolm Allison who, when I had dealings with him, seemed to be an arrogant man, although I can think of no row between us.

Manchester City v Leeds is the game that referees dread when the Football League monthly list arrives through the post! But you cannot ring up and say, 'I don't want that one. Give me something else.' Unless you are ill, you must go through with it.

I refereed one City v Leeds match and the conditions were slightly frosty. On the lunchtime TV programme Joe Mercer had made a joke about needing special studs ready for the action. It was an obviously light-hearted remark. Not long before the kick-off, Don Revie, the Leeds manager, came into my room and asked me to inspect the studs of the City players. This was before linesmen were required to check studs.

I did not look forward to going into the City dressing-room. But when I knocked and made the request, Allison replied, 'Yes, certainly.' There was nothing wrong with any of the players' studs. But over in the corner Francis Lee had a pair of miners' boots with steel toecaps and spikes. 'I'm going to wear these,' he said with a laugh. We all laughed.

'It was a joke,' said Allison. But it occurred to me that Leeds may not have thought so. Perhaps they suspected that Manchester City were pulling a fast one. Otherwise why would Revie had made the request?

In the world of professional football it seems that everyone suspects everyone else. The referee is the innocent party in the middle.

After another City match I came out of the dressing-room and saw Allison talking to some reporters on the other side of the passageway. 'What about the shirt pulling?' he shouted. I was willing to have a civil conversation but not to join in a shouting match across a passageway.

My next meeting with Allison was at a disciplinary hearing

after I had booked Mike Summerbee for a late tackle. Allison looked at me as though I were an imbecile. City brought film of the incident and played it in slow motion, showed stills and even played the film backwards. Summerbee lost his case. As Allison left the room where the hearing took place he said, 'It's a disgrace.' He was called back and lectured about his conduct.

In a City match against Derby I had trouble with the City captain, Colin Bell. Several players had gone down in unlikely circumstances and I was waving play on instead of letting the trainer come on. Bell fell down and said he was hurt. I thought he was all right and let the game continue. Bell just sat there. In the end I had to stop the game.

Off the field Bell is a quiet, inoffensive person, but he is not one of my favourite players to handle on the field. He is like some of the other City players: never happy with your decisions unless they suit him. He never stops talking to the referee.

Allison's team were at their worst in the City v Derby match at the end of the 1971–2 season. City had to win to stay in contention for the League title. There were 55,026 people at Maine Road that day. The City players constantly disagreed with me. I thought to myself : why don't I caution them?

No referee likes taking his book out unless he has to. I am not what is known as book happy. I was well down the bookings list that season. But a time comes when you have to say: 'That's enough. Any more from you and I'll caution you.'

City won 2–0 and one of their goals came from a penalty scored by Francis Lee. That season Lee scored from thirteen penalties in the League.

Lee creates problems for the referee because he is a 'flanneller' in the box. He goes down with a bump and immediately he is on to the referee, wanting a penalty. In many cases he puts on an act, and many referees recognize this. It is very hard, however, to sort out the genuine penalties. I was glad when that City v Derby match was over. It was the last game before I left for a trip to South Africa. I didn't want to get injured. I confess that my concentration might not have been as good as it should have been.

Out in South Africa I did twelve matches and got a good

Press. But after I left Malcolm Allison said 'You may think he's done well here but there are a lot of people in England who don't like him.' Ah well!

Rodney Marsh is a chatterbox on the field but he does it with a smile. He is one of the few players who give the appearance of enjoying himself while playing football. The majority seem to get no satisfaction out of what they are doing . . . unless they are winning.

Marsh talks a lot but I cannot remember him being much of a dissenter. One of the worst teams for dissenting in recent years was Arsenal. There was a period when their behaviour was exemplary, but the pressures of winning the Double had an adverse affect on them.

If a referee made a decision not to their liking they would hustle round him shouting and waving their arms. Frank McLintock always used to say a lot, and even some of the quiet men like Peter Simpson and George Armstrong would join in on occasions. I felt some sympathy for them. The tensions must have been immense, but I still think it is wrong to react in this way.

When I did the Arsenal v Manchester United match early in 1973 I blew for a free kick when Brian Kidd brought down Alan Ball. Now Kidd was never a rough player, but little George Armstrong – one of the quietest, best-behaved players in the Football League – rushed up and shouted, 'You're the hard man. You like dishing it out. We'll get you!'

To me, this is unbelievable. Why say anything? The foul had been spotted. Arsenal had their free kick. The game was about to get under way again. All this kind of talk does is to inflame passions and endanger the peace. Perhaps the explanation is that players are so keyed up that they do not realize what they say in the midst of the battle!

The Arsenal v Manchester United match was where I cautioned Tony Young of Manchester United for dangerous play. He caught John Radford in the face. Radford, who is sometimes quick-tempered, adopted a threatening attitude and I had to book him as well.

I don't like booking players. I think to myself: have I missed something earlier which, if I had spotted it, would have prevented this latest business following on? I have a conscience about it.

I think the real professional is the man who can control himself in such moments. That is the mark of professionalism for me – walking away from provocation and letting the referee deal with it.

Referees have been too lenient with the dissenters and chat merchants. They should have cracked down on them the way they did the players who tackled from behind. The best solution would be for the managers and coaches to take action themselves. They know it goes on. In a few cases it is a planned operation. But if the manager said he would not tolerate it any more, and anyone arguing with the referee would be fined in future, dissent would stop at that club.

If every act of dissenting and gamesmanship were picked up by referees, the number of bookings would treble; but the task would be impossible. The play-actors can be stopped too. Steve Kindon, the Wolves winger, kept hitting the ground in a spectacular manner in a match I refereed against Blackpool and it was obvious to me that he was acting. After the third time I said, 'If you take a dive like that again I will book you for ungentlemanly conduct.' Kindon stayed on his feet for the rest of the match!

There was a most peculiar incident before the Leeds v Birmingham City First Division game in 1972 which shows what some professionals in the game are thinking about each other. An hour before the kick-off I encountered one of the Birmingham defenders striding up the pitch. He seemed to be measuring it.

'Freddie Goodwin, our manager, has asked me to see if one half is longer than the other,' he said. I was thunderstruck. Surely Mr Goodwin couldn't believe that a club would deliberately make one half longer than the other half! What would be the purpose?

The player said he thought one half was six yards shorter than the other. Of course there was nothing I could do about it. I had no tape-measure on me of that length!

Later, Goodwin came in and asked me if I knew about the business of the pitch. I said I did and would be reporting it. He then left.

The game was played in the normal manner and there was nothing in the way Birmingham played to indicate that their defeat was due to the alleged irregular measurements. I had to report the affair to the Football League, but I heard no more about it.

An interesting case of alleged play-acting came in the Leeds v Spurs First Division match at Elland Road on 6 January. Millions of TV viewers had the chance to see it themselves on the following Sunday afternoon. As the ball was played into the right-hand side of the Spurs penalty area, Alan Gilzean chased it with Johnny Giles, the Leeds midfield player. The two men collided and Giles rolled over. Gilzean claimed he hadn't touched him. Giles shouted for a penalty. The referee awarded a penalty and Leeds scored from it.

Afterwards Bill Nicholson, the Spurs manager, said Giles had conned the referee into it. So did the Spurs players. All I say is this: if Giles did lay it on, were his actions in the right spirit of the game?

The players should have a duty to abide by the laws and play within the laws, not abuse them. It is hard enough for the referee to make a decision when everything is straight and open, let alone when the players are making things much worse than they really are.

The other type of gamesmanship which is now part of football in Britain is time-wasting by the team which is leading and wants to stop the other side equalizing. There are so many subtle versions of this that I am sure most football fans do not realize it is going on.

Here are some examples:

The winger takes a corner. He deliberately places the ball outside the quadrant at the corner flag. The linesman waves his flag. The referee comes over and tells the player to put the ball inside the quadrant. The player makes a show of placing the ball inside the arc. The crowd boo. They think the referee and linesmen are being officious. They miss the real design of the enterprise: to waste a few more seconds.

A goalkeeper takes a goal kick. He puts the ball down a foot outside the goal area after making all kinds of elaborate attempts to stamp the turf into the best position to take the ball. The linesman raises his flag. The referee, standing in the centre circle, waves the goalkeeper back. The goalkeeper pretends he doesn't know what the referee means. He looks at the linesman. The linesman holds his hands to signify the ball and moves them back a foot. The goalkeeper nods. He moves the ball back and walks to the start of his run. Again the crowd boo the officials and miss the goalkeeper's deliberate time-wasting.

One side is awarded a throw-in. A player comes up to take it. After a second or two of examining the options he decides there is nothing on. He throws the ball to an approaching colleague. The new man makes several trial runs but he too finds no one to throw at. So he gives the ball to a third player who eventually throws the ball in.

A player attended by a defender runs the ball over the touchline and concedes a throw-in. Instead of leaving the ball he kicks it twenty yards inside the field to where the referee is standing. The referee picks the ball up and has to throw it back to the defender waiting to take the throw. What does the referee want with the ball? Is he going to take the throw himself? It is time-wasting.

There was a good example of time-wasting at a Norwich v Leeds game in 1973. Norwich were awarded a throw and Allan Clarke picked up the ball and walked twenty yards with it outstretched in his hand to give it to the Norwich player waiting on the line to take the throw. The crowd applauded. They thought this was a sporting gesture. But why couldn't Clarke throw the ball back? Why walk twenty paces?

Players reply that they often have to slow things down at a free kick or throw-in because if they didn't the other side would take it before they were in position and a goal could result. But if the players taking the kicks and throws acted in the spirit of the laws they wouldn't make an attempt to take advantage.

If a forward went behind the by-line to collect the ball for a goal kick, the goalkeeper would wait until he was on the field and in position before the kick was taken. Well, that is how it should be. But professional football has reached a stage where such acts of sportsmanship are almost unknown.

When a shot went in the side netting and the referee

mistakenly signalled a goal in a Chelsea v Ipswich match, there were Chelsea players who wanted to claim a goal.

My son went on an FA coaching course, and one of the things he was taught was to stand on the ball at a free kick to prevent it being taken quickly. The Football League have since clamped down on this practice. Youngsters watching professionals in action copy the tricks of the trade. The bad example at the top goes right the way down through the different levels of the game, making it harder for inexperienced referees at the bottom of the scale to control players.

Time-wasting is a bookable offence and I have cautioned a number of players for it. But it is so underhand that often even the best referees can do little about stopping some of the less obvious dodges. You can shout yourself hoarse saying, 'Come on, get on with it!'

The spark goes out of the game when one side is intent on holding on. The crowd begins to lose interest. I am sure that this is yet another reason for the decline in attendances. Supporters want to see ninety minutes of action, not sixty minutes of action and thirty minutes of killing time.

One of the least interesting spectacles at a football match is the procedure which teams go through when a free kick is given near the penalty area. Twenty-one players are usually back for the kick and the defenders form a four-or five-man wall on the nearside post.

This takes time because another player has to form the wall up in line with the post, with the goalkeeper directing operations from his line. Inevitably the wall is less than ten yards from the ball and the referee has to order the defenders back. They move half a yard. But they must know it is still not ten yards. Most players know what ten pounds are, but not ten yards!

When the wall is eventually back where it should be, the observant referee might find that another source of irritation has arrived – the ball is no longer where he put it. The player taking the free kick has moved it a yard so that he now has a clear vision of the goal behind the wall. Graham Paddon, the Norwich midfield player who is one of the best dead-ball kickers in the First Division, confessed to doing this for one of his goals from a free kick. This is gamesmanship because it means that the defending side has been put at a serious disadvantage. They will probably have noticed that the ball has been moved and will be shouting protests. More trouble for the poor referee!

The referee has to stop his watch for time-wasting the same way he does for injuries. This is usually the explanation when the second half appears to go well beyond the forty-five minutes and yet the trainers have not been on the pitch.

This causes controversy because if a goal is scored in this extra time the players and manager of the aggrieved side will complain bitterly and the referee will be in trouble. This happened at the West Ham v WBA game in 1973 when referee Mike Kerkhof added on seven minutes for time-wasting and West Ham's winning goal came in this time.

If the innocent side scores then your feeling is that justice is done. But what if the guilty side scores the winning goal? That is how time-wasting can be so anger-provoking.

As an observer of soccer trends in the last twenty-five years, I have noticed some nasty things creeping into the game in the final years of my League career. For example, is it really necessary for Charlie George to give the crowd the V-sign? Does Peter Osgood have to do it? When several big stars like these have been seen to do it on television, you find it happening in Third and Fourth Division matches. Soon, footballers in the parks are doing it to each other. It cannot be a good thing for the image of the game.

The game is spattered with indecencies. Dave Gaskell, the Manchester United goalkeeper, and Jimmy Dunne, the Fulham defender, were summoned to court for taking their shorts down.

Asa Hartford, the Scottish international who plays for West Bromwich Albion, was fined £50 for spitting at a spectator at Norwich. Alan Ball, the former Preston manager, jumped over a barrier and exchanged blows with a supporter who angered him.

All these things happen through lack of control on the part of individuals. It is a high-pressure life, being in professional football, but not that high, surely? Suppose referees suddenly started lashing out at players who screamed abuse at them? Or gave the V-sign?

Some players need the kind of control that referees have to exercise in every match they take part in. The game would be better for it.

I have dwelt on the bad side of the modern game because I believe passionately that there are so many things that need putting right. But on the other side, there are still many teams who do not waste time or try to con the referee, clubs like West Ham, Tottenham Hotspur, Derby County, Burnley and Liverpool.

A Liverpool v West Ham encounter at Anfield in 1971-2 was a dream match. Twenty minutes went by before the first foul was awarded. I must have made only half-a-dozen decisions of any consequence in the whole game. There was no dissent. The game kept moving and whenever I gave the advantage, it was accepted by the players.

Bobby Moore, the England and West Ham captain, hardly says a word during a match, certainly not to the referee. Never when I have refereed a match in which his team were taking part can I recall one single word from him. Not even at the start when I shake hands with him.

'Good afternoon Mr Moore,' I would say. He might have smiled occasionally but he never said anything.

Derby have a strict disciplinary code within their club, and manager Brian Clough fines players who are suspended by the FA Disciplinary Committee. Roy McFarland, the England centre-half, was fined by Clough in the 1972-3 season. Derby provide a good example of a team taking its lead from the manager. I cannot recall being involved in any unpleasantness at a match at the Baseball Ground.

D

4

The hard men

Some players are harder to referee than others. Two of them were in the England side in 1972–3 – Peter Storey of Arsenal and Norman Hunter of Leeds. They are both hard men.

I do not use the word 'hard' when I mean 'dirty'. Neither of these players is dirty in the sense that they deliberately go on to the field with the intention of harming an opponent. But they are so competitive, so determined to win, so aggressive that some of their tackles which start off as good tackles end up in the black book.

The test of a real hard man is whether he can take it as well as give it out. Dave Mackay, the toughest player in my time, could take it. I had trouble with him on many occasions. An incident between Mackay and Billy Bremner, the Leeds captain, made the sports picture of the year. It showed Mackay grabbing Bremner by the shirt and threatening him. I was the referee. It was the third minute of the match and Bremner tackled Mackay. Mackay leaped to his feet and seized Bremner's shirt front – a ridiculous response, I thought. The foul had been given; there was no need for him to do anything or say anything. But that was Mackay's weakness. He was an explosive character.

Both Mackay and Bremner spoke in such broad Scots that I couldn't understand what they were saying. Though I have sent players off for using abusive language at me, I do not mind swearing among players. The football field is the foot-baller's factory and if he can't swear there, where can he swear? I do not swear myself on the field, though some referees – Gordon Hill is one – use barrack-room language when they feel like giving vent to their feelings.

Mackay's aggressive attitude was such that often he would get the ball in a tackle so recklessly that his opponent would be flattened.

I have had a few rucks with Bremner in my time. He used to be very fiery earlier in his career but has now cooled down considerably.

Unlike Dave Mackay, Hunter is not the kind of player who likes being tackled himself. When I refereed an FA Cup Tie, he was tackled hard from behind and rushed up to me to complain bitterly. I thought it was a fairy touch of a tackle.

Some of Hunter's tackles are frightening. I know because I have been a yard or two away from some of them. Sometimes he goes in so hard it is difficult to distinguish his intent.

I sometimes think he has been booked less times than he deserved because of his attitude after he has committed a foul. Inevitably his hands will be held up like a soldier surrendering and he will be smiling. He will apologize and be nice about it. But what is the point of apologizing once you have fouled someone? Far better not to have fouled in the first place!

Hunter is one of the few players I know off the field, and he is a nice fellow – a perfect gentleman and pleasant to talk to. Peter Storey has a similar style to Hunter, and like Hunter he is a difficult man for a referee to handle. But I have always found that I could control Storey verbally.

My first decision in the Arsenal v Manchester United match in the 1972–3 season was for a foul in the third minute. Storey came charging up like a fierce tribal warrior.

'That was never a foul,' he said. I never believe in getting upset myself. I walk slowly towards the player. If I race up I add to the confusion. The player thinks I am het up as well as he.

I went up to Storey and said, 'Look, we've been out here exactly three minutes. We might as well pack up now if we're going to behave like that.'

After that he never spoke to me again. You have to stamp

on this kind of thing right at the start. If you don't, you have a battle on your hands.

I do not believe in eyeball-to-eyeball confrontations. I never try and stare someone out. If I have to book a player I go up to him and say in my normal voice, 'What is your name?' The usual reaction is: 'You know my name.' I reply that I don't. Often I don't know who the players are, especially outside the First Division. It is not my business to know who the players are. I am looking at their feet, where they are likely to run to, their arms . . . just as much as their faces. After he gives his name I say, 'And the initial?' I say, 'I am officially cautioning you.' Then I state the offence.

I have no book as such. You read that, 'Norman Hunter went into referee Norman Burtenshaw's book', but I never use one. I have a black, plastic cover with half a postcard inside on which I jot down names.

Some referees note the names of the two teams, which side won the toss, which way they kicked and the score. I committed all those things to memory. The less the 'book' came out the better, I thought.

One of the players I had to caution was Peter Osgood of Chelsea. You could never take your eyes off him. He was responsible for a lot of niggling fouls off the ball, like the one I booked him for in the 1971 League Cup Final against Stoke.

Stoke centre-half Denis Smith was lying on the ground and Osgood could easily have stepped over him. But he stepped on him. Osgood later appealed to a FA Disciplinary Commission . . . and lost.

Osgood's actions off the ball – like jostling opponents in the wall – earned him a reputation which may have affected his England career. The FA Disciplinary Committee once directed that his disciplinary record should be sent to the England team manager, Sir Alf Ramsey. That meant only one thing – the Committee wanted Ramsey to take Osgood's record into account and weigh the possible consequences of picking him again for international football. Osgood's disciplinary shortcomings possibly prevented him from becoming one of the all-time greats, because he had the ability.

Some footballers became known as players that referees have to watch because their eyesight was so poor that it

36

affected the timing of their tackles. I am sure this was why Nobby Stiles was guilty of so many late tackles in his career. Nobby was a fearsome fellow for a referee to handle. He was so aggressive – toothless, almost snarling. He gave me the impression that he loathed referees. Perhaps he did. Off the field he was a different person, quiet and diffident. He looked like Woody Allen in his horn-rimmed spectacles.

Derek Jefferson, one of the dozen players I sent off in my eleven years, also suffered from defective eyesight. I ordered him off once in a match against Chelsea for a tackle on Alan Birchenall. It was a bad foul.

Another player I sent off was Bobby Kellard, the much-travelled midfield player who played for Southend, Crystal Palace, Portsmouth, Ipswich, Leicester and Bristol City. He was a hard little nut who liked to mix it. He struck an opponent and I had a clear view. When I said 'Off!' he walked away without a word. Later, in the dressing-room, I said to the linesmen, 'You saw what happened with Kellard, didn't you?' They replied they hadn't seen a thing. That was amazing. Neither of the linesmen had seen Kellard sent off. I had never known that before. But it can happen.

No referee likes stopping a game and giving lectures to offending players. He prefers to run quietly up behind the offender and say what he has to say. The player gets the message and the game continues without the crowd knowing much about the incident. A good example of this came in a match at the Dell, Southampton, in the 1972-3 season. The player concerned was Brian O'Neil, the Southampton wing-half who has a very long list of cautions in his career.

O'Neil was fouled and got up angrily. He hared back after the player who had kicked him, his eyes blazing. I ran with him all the way. It must have looked funny. I didn't say a word. But by the time O'Neil caught the other player up he knew the score. Nothing more happened.

John McGrath, O'Neil's colleague in the Southampton side, had problems with referees but he was not a dirty player. He had a habit of taking man and ball, and was frequently penalized for it.

Certain things that happen on a football pitch are inexplicable to the fans on the terraces. In one West Ham game, Billy

Bonds was fouled but kept his feet and I allowed him the advantage. He went on and shot and the goalkeeper made a fine save. It was a good effort. As he turned away, an opposing player said something. I wasn't close enough to hear what it was but Bonds spat in the other player's face. I had no alternative but to send Bonds off. He was going through a bad time just then.

After the game he came into my room. 'No hard feelings,' he said. He appealed against the sending off, but lost. I never had any more trouble with Billy Bonds. I felt sorry for him. Just one antagonizing remark and he lost his head.

Something which bothered most referees during the sixties was Jackie Charlton's tactic of standing on the goal line in front of the goalkeeper at corner kicks. Was it permissible? I thought that on some occasions Charlton jumped before the ball arrived to obstruct the vision of the goalkeeper. When he did that I penalized him.

But there were other occasions when he jumped at the right time and headed goals. No referee could penalize him then. I like Charlton as a person. He was another aggressive player. If he disagreed with a decision he would come at you in a short sharp blast. He wouldn't keep on.

Later, of course, coaches devised more ways of putting the goalkeeper off, such as telling a short player to stand close to the goalkeeper and walk into him. But if the referee took up the right position – close to the post, behind the by-line – he could spot all these things.

One of the players who never gave referees a respite was Terry Neill, the Northern Ireland, Arsenal and Hull centre-half and former Professional Footballers' Association chairman. There was an amazing change in him when he left Arsenal to join Hull City as player-manager. I never knew another player who adopted such a persistent verbal attitude towards a referee. He had something to say about every decision – not violently or in a manner which constituted a breach of the laws, but in a way which, after a while, got on my nerves. He said referees were after him and that he was a marked man. I certainly wasn't after him, but his attitude annoyed me. A referee can only take so much of that.

Towards the end of the sixties the emphasis changed towards

acceptance of the hard men. The Hunters and the Storeys were talked about the way Tom Finney and Stan Matthews had been talked about in the forties and fifties. Nearly every team had its so-called ball winner. I am not qualified to say whether this is a bad thing or a good thing for the game. With teams tending to play possession football, certainly someone has to win the ball.

In my early days it was traditional for a defender to go in hard against the outstanding ball player in the other side, either to slow him down or put some doubt in his mind about the advisability of playing his usual game. This 'quietening' foul would take place in the first few minutes. It happened so early that many referees were reluctant to take action. The aggressor achieved his aim. The forward swallowed any bravery he might have had left and played no more effective part in the game.

Today this no longer happens. The standard of refereeing is higher and the Football League has encouraged referees to caution players who infringe, however early in the game. Those players who commit violent conduct – whether in the first minute or the last or at any other time – are automatically sent off. The ball player has a chance of expressing his skills; unfortunately there seem to be fewer of these players about.

The players say the worst foul they know is the 'over-the-top' tackle. I did not see many examples of this in my career and I think its importance was over-emphasized. The worst foul, I thought, was the so-called professional foul. Hoodlum foul would be a better expression. When a skilful player beat his opponents through sheer skill, got into position to shoot and was deliberately hacked down from behind – that was the worst foul, to my mind.

The answer from the players was: 'What could we do? It would have meant a goal. I couldn't do anything else. It was the last resort.' We heard this a number of times on television. Managers condoned it. Even TV commentator David Coleman has said, 'he had to do it'.

In my view, this type of foul was one of the reasons why attendances declined so rapidly in the early seventies. The players were robbing themselves of a living. Fans stayed away because they wanted more goals. But the players, by fouling opponents who were in good scoring positions, prevented goals. When this kind of foul happened four times in a match, twice at each end, instead of the final score being 2–2 it was 0–0. The players may have complimented themselves on earning a point. But could they really be proud of the way they did it?

I wonder what the majority of fans thought at the 1971 League Cup Final when the Chelsea forward Chris Garland made a run on the right and was beautifully positioned to threaten the Stoke goal. Stoke defender Mike Pejic ran straight into him, and the chance disappeared.

What happens after the 'professional' foul? The game stops. That irritates the fans for a start. The referee has to lecture the offender, in all probability caution him for ungentlemanly conduct. Then there is the pantomime of getting the defending side ten yards from the ball for the free kick. The Football League tried to prevent the deliberate holding up of free kicks by defenders encroaching, but despite their entreaties referees are still unable to get free kicks taken smoothly and quickly around the box.

The scramble of players in and around the wall was undignified and bad for the game. I don't think the managers and players who spoke up for the professional foul considered this point.

Next to the professional foul I place the sneak foul, the infringement which takes place off the ball. I believe some coaches instruct their players in certain techniques, such as taking opponents out. This means deliberately obstructing a player who is making a good run into a position away from the ball. Spectators watching the ball may not notice this. If they see a player on the ground they think there has been an accident. They do not know the truth.

This obstruction often happens at a free kick where several players make decoy runs. A key man suddenly finds himself crashing into an opponent and the move is defeated.

Because these fouls were on the increase I adopted a new positional system. I adapted the diagonal system to one that resembled half a swastika – down one touchline, across the centre of the pitch and down the touchline on the other half of the pitch. This enabled me to stay outside the play so that I

Leeds v Arsenal at Elland Road 1971. Burtenshaw points to the centre.
Jackie Charlton's goal counts and Arsenal's players are enraged. Lining
up to protest are skipper Frank McLintock, Peter Simpson and Pat Rice.
The man in white with arms upraised is Leeds skipper Billy Bremner.

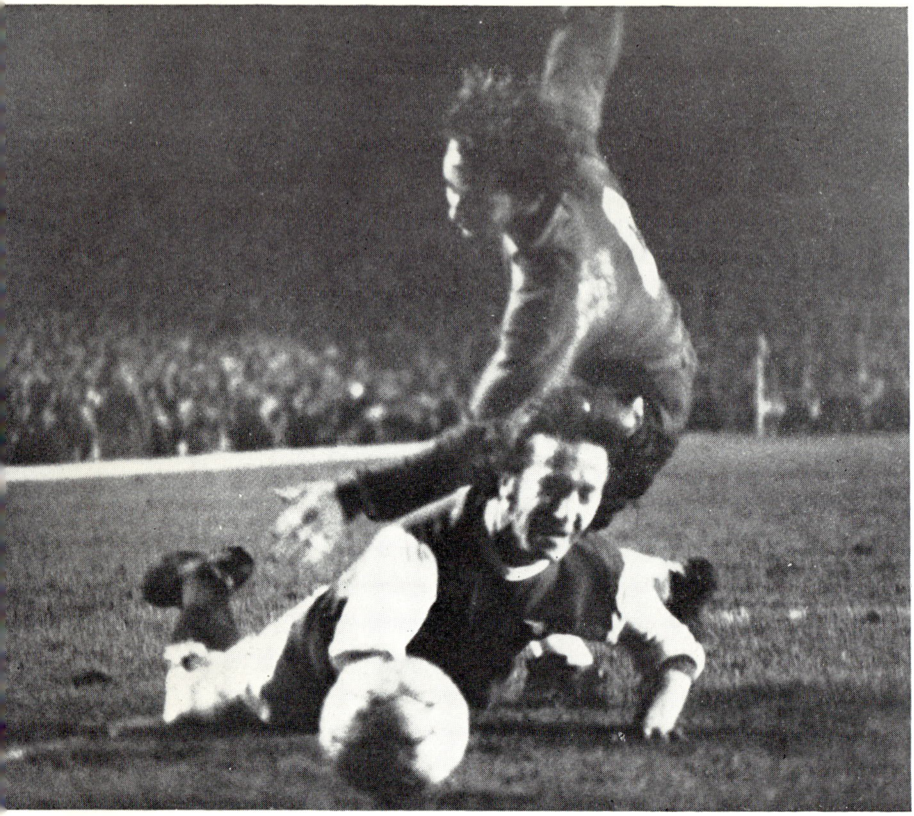

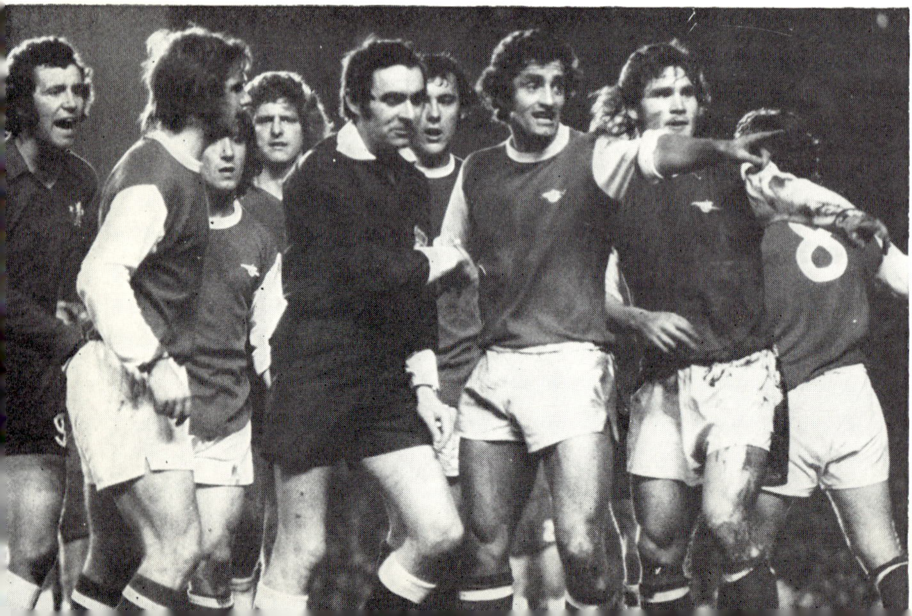

Above: Not all European matches attract big crowds. This European match at the San Siro stadium in Milan (capacity 90,000) refereed by Burtenshaw was watched by only 3,000!

Above left: The incident that caused the row in the Arsenal v Chelsea FA Cup replay in 1973. Steve Kember (Chelsea) brings down George Armstrong (Arsenal). Is it inside or outside the penalty area?

Below left: 'The linesman wants to see you,' says Arsenal skipper Frank McLintock. It's the Arsenal v Chelsea FA Cup replay at Highbury. Referee Burtenshaw gives Arsenal a free kick outside the penalty area but after speaking to the linesman, gives a penalty.
'It was the only time I changed my mind,' he says.

Above: Spurs v a Japanese XI. Spurs players Martin Chivers, Phil Beal and Peter Collins accept the decision without a murmur.

Below: Spurs winger Jimmy Neighbour's next trick is to beat Norman Burtenshaw on the outside! The Japanese are becoming increasingly interested in soccer.

could see as much of the game as possible. If you are in the middle of the pitch facing the play you can miss what is going on behind you.

These are some of the sneak fouls that crept into the English game from the Continent long before Britain entered the Common Market in 1973:

The hand off: two players running for the same ball – one gains possession because at the vital moment he has shoved the other away with his arm.

Shirt pulling: the same situation. The attacker who gets there first loses the advantage of being first because he finds his shirt half-ripped off his back.

The centre-forward backing into the centre-half when they go up for a ball; the centre-half leaning on the centre-forward.

A player reaches out his hand to ruffle an opponent's hair after bringing him down. But he doesn't ruffle it; he pulls it.

The defender who appears to be picking up an opponent but in reality is pinching him in a painful way. This happened to England international Mike Channon in the 1972–3 season and he was sent off for retaliating. You can understand the provocation he was under. The FA Disciplinary Committee took no further action when his case came up later.

Players slyly elbowing each other at free kicks; this became a particular problem when English teams began copying the Brazilians and placed attackers in the other team's defensive wall.

Referees have a thankless task deciding who elbowed whom. There was a good example of this when Chelsea left-back Ron Harris was ordered off at Brighton in a Third Round FA Cup tie in January 1973.

Two players jostling each other at a corner. When this happens I usually say, 'Is it vitally important that you two stand on the same blade of grass?'

All these niggling fouls build up the tension. The player who has been surreptitiously elbowed is likely to retaliate with a punch. Before the referee can apportion blame he has an explosive incident on his hands. In modern football such incidents are not left to the two players concerned. In a moment, a dozen or more players are milling around pushing and shoving each other. It is very difficult for the referee to sort out the guilty from the innocent. I find it hard to understand why other players want to get involved.

Like good defenders, referees do not follow the ball. They watch for as many things as possible. There are twenty-two players in a match, not just the one who is in possession. Experience teaches a referee to anticipate where the ball is going and what is happening when other players are making what the coaches call blindside runs.

For example, I never watch the flight of a clearance from a goalkeeper or a long goal-kick. What is the point? I know where the ball is going. What I should be concentrating on is what is happening where the ball is going to land. Is the defender pushing from behind? Is the attacker leaning on? You need all your concentration to determine the facts.

I find some players are easy to 'read'. You can make your runs because you know where they are going to pass the ball. I put Alan Ball of England and Arsenal in this category. He is fairly predictable.

Bobby Moore, the England and West Ham captain, is the opposite. Moore is thoroughly unpredictable. I am never at ease when I referee his games. Some of his passes are most unorthodox, and a referee can be caught going in the wrong direction. This happened in a FA Cup tie at Hull early in 1973. Goalkeeper Bobby Ferguson was also caught out, for he fumbled the ball and it led to Hull's only goal.

Sneak fouls came into the professional game because the people in it got further and further from the ideal of playing within the true spirit of the laws of the game. Whenever I spoke to a player about the spirit of the game the usual reply would be: 'What spirit? I've got a living to make.'

Is it possible to play all out to win and keep within the spirit of the game? I believe it is. There are many players who do this. Bobby Moore is a leading example. So was Bobby Charlton.

The perfect professional to my mind is Pat Jennings, the Spurs and Northern Ireland goalkeeper. I never knew him object to a decision. On and off the field he is a gentleman.

The Derby players are well behaved. Colin Todd is immaculate. And so is Peter Simpson of Arsenal. He came from the same village as me and we know each other well. I only heard him complain once, and that was during the row following the Jackie Charlton goal at Elland Road which Arsenal claimed was offside. Chris Lawler, the Liverpool right-back, is a gentleman. His colleague Steve Heighway, who started his career as an amateur, is another player with a commendable attitude.

Heighway is chopped down countless times during a season, often in a spectacular fashion because he is a very quick player. But there are never any tantrums from him. He doesn't jump up shouting angrily and demanding that the referee book the offender.

Martin Chivers, the Spurs and England centre-forward, is probably subject to more provocation than most players, but he too is always calm and disciplined, a model player to referee.

None of these players tugs shirts, takes opponents out or pinches people. None of them has to; each is a good enough player to succeed in the game purely on his skill.

5

The Millwall affair

On the afternoon of Saturday, 14 October 1967, I was leaving
the field at the end of the Millwall v Aston Villa match when
I was knocked down and kicked by some young men who had
invaded the pitch. It was an incident that nearly brought about
the first-ever strike by referees.

Our Association met a few days later and passed a resolu-
tion saying that no referee would go to the Den again until
'plans for eliminating encroachment are fully implemented'.

Youngsters running on to the pitch had developed into a
habit after England won the World Cup in 1966. There was
plenty to get excited about. People thought it was a good idea :
youngsters showing their exuberance. When a goal was scored
the player who put the ball into the net would be mobbed.

Soon it was realized that it might not be a good idea after
all. Perhaps those fans were not merely expressing their joy;
they might be upset about something. Club officials were
worried and so were referees. They would be powerless if some
of these fans decided to attack a referee or a player. In the year
following the World Cup there were four separate incidents of
referees being molested. Nothing was done about it.

The matter was raised with the Chairman of the FA, Dr (as
he then was) Andrew Stephen, at the 32nd annual conference
of the Association of Football League Referees and Linesmen.
One questioner said referees had even been killed in some
countries abroad. What action was the FA taking? Dr Stephen
said the FA was very concerned about this problem and was

taking steps to 'meet anything in this direction which might lift its ugly head in the future'.

There was a crowd of 13,392 at the Den that 14 October, which meant the ground was about a third full. I enjoyed going to the Den. It had a good atmosphere and the supporters there seemed to relish their football. I booked three players – Charlie Aitken of Villa and Eamonn Dunphy and Keith Weller of Millwall.

It was not a violent match. Villa were leading 2–1 when, fifteen minutes from time, I awarded Millwall a free kick. Dunphy took it and from his pass the substitute, Butch Howell, had his shot blocked on the line by a defender. The Millwall players appealed for hands and also claimed that the ball had crossed the line. I was in a good position to see that neither had happened, and I waved play on.

When I blew the final whistle the score was still 2–1 to Villa. Scores of fans rushed on. I did not think there was any hostility towards me. I was near the centre of the pitch. I picked up the ball and began walking towards the dead ball line. Suddenly I was knocked down from behind and as I fell the boot went in. I was kicked twice, once in the groin and once in the leg. I was certain that this was no accident. I was conscious but in excruciating pain. I remember thinking to myself, 'If I get up it won't look so bad.' But I couldn't get up.

Police and St John's Ambulance men came to my assistance and helped me off the field. They put me on a table inside the passageway near the dressing-rooms and the pain gradually eased. After a few minutes I was able to get up and walk to the dressing-room. I felt better in the bath. Gordon Borland, the Millwall secretary, came in to see if I was all right. I said I was. I dressed and left the ground without seeing Benny Fenton, the Millwall manager, or Mr Mick Purser, the chairman. Outside, some reporters waited to know what had happened. I replied that it would be in my report to the Football League.

The Millwall programme had warned youngsters about running on to the pitch. 'If you don't take any notice of this warning we will have to charge you full admission,' said the editorial. Sometime before, the programme had warned about the possibility of the ground being closed if encroachment did not stop.

Obviously the club was worried about the problem. Its ground had been closed for a week in 1950. When the Press told Denis Follows about the latest incident, he said: 'If the facts are correct this is one of the most serious offences concerning a referee in recent times and must incur the gravest penalties.'

I was surprised to learn later that Millwall officials were trying to whitewash the affair. Mr Purser was quoted as saying: 'I thought he just fell down.' Another story was that I had fainted.

I felt unwell when I eventually arrived home by train and had to call my doctor. He gave me a sedative. That night I rang Mr George Readle, then secretary of the Referees and Linesmen Association, and Mr Stan Lover, the President. Both men had been concerned about encroachment at the annual conference. The next day Mr Lover asked the Football League for a meeting to discuss the question of the safety of referees.

Denis Howell, a former League referee himself and then Minister of Sport, said: 'Referees do a great job because they love it, and they must be given full protection. It is diabolical when you get clubs with a repeated history of misconduct. The punishment in such cases should be very high.'

I liked the comment of one Millwall fan, a Mr Cook of Wapping. 'Mr Burtenshaw was about the weakest referee I have ever seen,' he said. 'He seemed to pay little attention to his linesmen, and his weakness in handling the match in my opinion incensed these so-called supporters. I feel sorry for the club.'

I was worried by the whole business. I had only been on the League list for five years. I was a newcomer really. Now I was the centre of one of the biggest refereeing controversies of the decade.

On the Monday night I was due to take the Fulham v Workington Football League Cup replay at Craven Cottage. I rang the League on the Sunday and said I was fit enough to carry on. I was no hero, but I thought it was important to continue. If whoever had kicked me thought he had got away with it and stopped a referee taking a match, the next lout who wanted to put a referee out of action would be encouraged to follow his example.

I do not usually take my wife Dorothy with me to matches but I did that Monday night at Fulham. When I arrived at Craven Cottage the secretary, Graham Hortop, came up to me and said, 'We have had a call from someone saying he is going to shoot you.'

He said the police had been told about the threat but were not intending to give me an escort. They thought it came from a crank. I was not worried unduly. But no one was allowed into my dressing-room.

When I came out for the start of the match there was spontaneous applause from the 8,614 crowd. I thought that was a tribute for referees generally, not me in particular. I think those people realized that refereeing could be a hazardous job.

Meanwhile another referee, Harry New of Portsmouth, was being escorted off the pitch by six policemen at the Den after controlling the Millwall v Northampton match. Denis Follows was in the stand at the Den, and though 150 fans invaded the pitch at the end, there were no incidents.

Two days after the Fulham game the Football League Referees' and Linesmen's Association circulated a questionnaire to all its members to find out how many encroaching incidents there had been in the season. There were questions like:

Were you at any time in danger of being molested?
Did you get police protection?
How many police were on the ground?

The general view was that not enough was being done by clubs to stop encroachment and the executive wanted facts to put before the Football League.

The meeting with the League took place at Lytham St Annes on 2 November, and the referees' delegates, Stan Lover and George Readle, asked the League representatives, Len Shipman, Sam Bolton, Bob Lord, Alan Hardaker and Eric Howarth, what positive steps were to be taken. Mr Shipman replied that a Commission would look into the Millwall affair on 9 November and would meet at the Den.

Mr Lover and Mr Readle said that clubs should think about raising boundary walls to stop youngsters climbing over,

47

penning spectators in and restricting movement from one part of the ground to another, and having more patrols at points where fans were known to come on to the pitch. They also felt that police should escort officials off at the end. This has now become standard practice. Indeed, most of the safety suggestions made at that meeting by the referees were later adopted.

The Football Association asked my doctor, the late Dr Michael Evans, to come with me to the Commission which met in the Millwall boardroom on 9 November. No doubt they wanted him because his medical evidence differed somewhat from that given by the Millwall doctor.

My report was presented to the three-man Commission (Noel Watson, a JP from Nottingham Forest, Len Shipman and Frank Davis). The report read:

I have to report on an incident involving the referee of the match (Millwall v Villa). After signalling the end of the game, several hundred spectators rushed on to the pitch, ignoring a public-address warning to stay off.

I was escorted off the pitch by several police officers. We were jostled by the spectators. I was then tripped from behind and whilst on the ground received blows, one of which was in the stomach.

The police then assisted me from the ground and I received treatment from the St John's Ambulance men and the club doctor. After one hour I was escorted from the ground by police.

The Commission also had the reports of the two linesmen. Mr G. E. Palmer said in his:

I have to report an incident that occurred after the above match with Mr N. Burtenshaw. After the final whistle the crowd swarmed on to the pitch in spite of the police and public-address asking them to keep off, and one spectator approached Mr Burtenshaw. The police hustled this spectator away and a number of policemen surrounded Mr Burtenshaw. I moved towards the tunnel ahead of Mr Burtenshaw and a group of spectators were jostling the Millwall goalkeeper.

The police forced this group out of my way. As I reached the tunnel I realized Mr Burtenshaw was not following, and I went back only to find Mr Burtenshaw in great pain and being carried by the police. I did not see the actual assault. After attention for about fifteen minutes by St John's Ambulance men, Mr Burtenshaw was helped to the referee's changing-room.

Mr M. Kerkhof's report said:

It was agreed before the match that I would officiate at the dressing-room end of the ground. This would allow me to get away from the ground as quickly as possible after the final whistle.

I had arranged for a taxi to pick me up from the ground at 5 p.m. This would then allow me to collect my own car which was parked some distance away from Millwall.

The final whistle sounded at approximately 4.56 p.m. I, like all the players, ran towards the dressing-room. As I did so, many spectators jumped the walls and ran across the field in the direction of the players' exit. One or two collided with me, but I was sure it was accidental and thought no more about it. I passed through the tunnel and into the dressing-room.

I changed hurriedly. When I was half-dressed the door opened and in walked the gentleman to pay the officials. I inquired about my colleagues as they were taking rather a long time. The man said: 'There has been an accident and the referee has been hurt.'

Still half-dressed, I ran from my room towards the tunnel only to be stopped by the St John's Ambulance brigade. They asked me to return as it was nothing serious. I noticed that the referee was being attended to on a table just inside the tunnel.

I then spoke to Mr Burtenshaw who looked very dazed and was holding his head. Mr Burtenshaw told me he was OK and to get on my way. I then bid my colleagues farewell and left the ground.

Mr Purser, the Millwall chairman, made a statement which read:

E

As chairman of Millwall FC and for the good of football in general, I feel, in view of the grave distortion of facts by the National Press, that I should acquaint you with our version of what took place at the conclusion of the above match; without prejudice to any further statement the club will be submitting when we have had sight of the referee's report.

When Mr Burtenshaw blew his whistle to end the game, a large number of youngsters invaded the pitch in spite of the efforts of the police to restrain them. We feel that the majority of youths took this action more in a spirit of adventure than with any hostile intentions. Perhaps the fact that the game was televised provoked them to get in the act by mixing with the players and officials as they were leaving the playing-pitch.

With so many youngsters milling around it is possible that the referee was tripped accidentally or otherwise causing him to fall and unintentionally receiving a blow in the process. We have asked the police to make a full report of exactly what happened to the best of their knowledge from what they saw and from their interrogation of match officials and members of their own staff.

Referring again to the distortion of facts by the Press and the damaging effect this can have not only on the public but on the people in the game itself, I would like you to know that this morning we received a telephone call from Mr Bonsor, chairman of Watford FC, with an offer for the use of their ground in the event that this ground is closed. Bear in mind that this was received before the case had been dealt with by the FA. We feel that this is just one proof of the adverse impact Press reports such as appeared this week-end can have, where it would appear that the case has been prejudged.

Naturally we are very much concerned with events of this nature and the damage to the image of the game. We have done everything possible in an effort to prevent this sort of thing happening, but as with clubs all over the country, there seems to be no limit to which youngsters will go to provoke incidents at football grounds.

After reading my report, the Millwall club made a second statement:

Further to our chairman's letters to Mr Follows, we are amazed by the allegation that Mr Burtenshaw was the victim of an attack by supporters. From evidence obtained from members of our staff and a reliable source such as the police, we are of the opinion that in the confusion Mr Burtenshaw is mistaken as to what took place.

When Mr Burtenshaw signalled the end of the game he was approximately three-quarters of the pitch-length away from the players' tunnel. A number of youngsters did invade the pitch in spite of the efforts of the police to restrain them. We contend that these boys did so in order to get themselves in on the act, as this particular match was being televised. In our opinion, had there been any hostile intentions on the part of the youngsters towards the referee, then any such offence would have occurred close to the spot where Mr Burtenshaw was standing soon after he ended the game. As it was, he approached the players' tunnel where he was surrounded by a cordon of police. He did appear to slip, but from the evidence of eye-witnesses and the police no blows were struck. Our Medical Officer's report, enclosed herewith, in our opinion supports this. We have applied for a copy of the police report, but I understand that we are unlikely to receive this. I understand, however, that in all probability the FA, as the authority inquiring into this case, would be provided with a copy if they so desired. We feel that in fairness to this club such a copy should be obtained.

In view of the adverse publicity and the attacks made against this club by certain sections of the Press as a result of this incident, may we please be granted a personal hearing when this case comes up.

When the cross-examination started, I was asked by Mr Purser, 'Did you faint?' I said I had nothing to add to my report. The Millwall evidence was inconclusive. Their officials said they had seen no blows struck.

Dr Yhapp, the Millwall doctor, was cross-examined on his report in which he stated that he had applied a cold compress to my stomach. Mr Follows asked him, 'Do you usually apply a cold compress to someone's stomach when they have fainted?'

There were differences between his report and that of my own doctor. The Millwall doctor said in his:

I saw Mr Burtenshaw lying on a stretcher, much to my surprise, as I had seen him walking off the pitch through the tunnel.

He was conscious. His eyes were tightly closed, hands placed over the lower part of the abdomen. His colour was good; he was not sweating; his respiration was normal, his pulse was fair in volume and was ninety per minute. I undid his shorts and examined for injury to his testicles and inguinal hernia but could find no abnormality. I examined the abdomen especially the lower part over which he had his hands. There was no sign of bruising nor tenderness in the abdominal wall or internal organs.

My opinion was that Mr Burtenshaw had a slight faint and was recovering from it. There was no medical evidence that he had a severe physical injury. To hasten his recovery I put a cold compress on the lower abdomen. His pulse improved and I left after two minutes to have a look at the injuries of the footballers.

I did not consider that Mr Burtenshaw needed any further medical treatment. Five minutes after I returned from the players' dressing-rooms, Mr Burtenshaw was in his dressing-room having a bath. The door was still locked fifteen minutes afterwards, but the Millwall FC secretary, Mr D. G. Borland, said that he had talked with Mr Burtenshaw but he had not asked for any further medical assistance.

The evidence from Dr Michael Evans, my own doctor who examined me three days after the incident, was somewhat different. He wrote:

I saw this patient on 17 October and my findings were as follows.

There was a bruise one inch in diameter on the outer aspect of the right thigh.

There was a right direct inguinal hernia and around it the skin was red for a diameter of three inches.

He was in a tense and rather emotional state.

The first injury was compatible with having fallen, or received a blow, on the outer thigh. The signs of trauma on the front of the abdominal wall lying in a position halfway between the groin and the navel, would, in my opinion, have been caused by an impact between an object very approximately the size of the area showing signs of damage and the abdominal wall. Both injuries are in my opinion compatible with the history I obtained from him that he had been kicked in the two areas concerned. Mr Burtenshaw had also sought advice from one of my partners on Sunday, 15 October, as he was in a shaken condition and a sedative had been given.

The hearing lasted just over two hours. We were called back to hear the verdict – a fine of £1,000 on Millwall. The club was also ordered to post warning notices.

Nothing was said about how the club was to be compelled to stop invasions of the pitch in future. Mr Purser said the board were going to discuss putting up a fence. When it was finally erected it was little more than a pathetic gesture. It was hardly more than a foot high. No teenager would be stopped by it.

Some of my colleagues were furious about the verdict. Former World Cup referee Ken Aston said, 'I would have thought that the transference of £1 or £1,000 from Millwall to the FA will not do the slightest good or offer the slightest guarantee that the same thing cannot happen again. I think the proper punishment would have been to close the ground until Millwall could give an adequate and acceptable assurance that a repetition of the incident could not occur. A club which had to give such an assurance would be forced to put up fences. That is what I would have liked to see.'

Many referees agreed with those sentiments. I think some people at Millwall thought I was to blame for what happened. When my name was put forward to referee a match there on a later occasion the club objected. I never went back to the Den. I would have liked to. I had nothing against the club, its officials or its supporters.

Frankly, I thought the Millwall club could have done more for themselves at the Commission. If they had made some concrete proposals to put things right, the row that followed would have been avoided. Instead, they tried to make out that I hadn't been assaulted.

Stan Lover, President of the Referees and Linesmen Association, came to the hearing at the Den with me although he was not allowed in. He felt very strongly about the whole issue. Later that day he telephoned the Association secretary George Readle and the treasurer George Dutton. All three men agreed that the situation was unsatisfactory and it was time the referees spoke up.

In the twenty-four hours after the Millwall verdict Mr Lover spoke to most of the members of the executive and got their agreement to a statement that no referee would take a match at the Den until the ground was made safe. The statement, issued at 12.30 p.m. on the Friday, read:

> The officers of the Association of Football League Referees and Linesmen have considered the statement of the Commission of Enquiry held at Millwall FC yesterday and note with regret that it does not contain an assurance that immediate action will be taken to provide adequate protection for players and match officials from interference by members of the public at this ground.
>
> The Association is firmly of the opinion that unless positive steps are taken to isolate spectators from the field of play, encroachment will continue and the possibility of tragic consequences will become a reality.
>
> The Association has therefore informed the Football League that it is advising its members not to officiate at the Millwall FC until such time as the plans for eliminating encroachment are fully implemented.

It was the first time the referees had let the Football League know they had a collective mind of their own. As a member of the executive, I was in favour of the statement. I felt that we had to take this stand not because of what happened at Millwall but because the same thing could happen at any ground. Not enough was being done to safeguard referees.

The Association is no trade union. Once the executive make a decision, it does not follow that the members have to obey it. But in the hours that followed the issuing of the statement

54

there was solidarity among the referees. Only a few disagreed.

I deplored a statement by the FIFA referee Kevin Howley, who said he was thinking of resigning from the Association because he had not been consulted.

I have spoken up against encroachment for some years past (he said). And I have said this sort of thing would finish up with a manslaughter or a murder charge. And I have been an advocate of a two-week strike by referees. But I could not support the enmity of one club and one ground. We are looking for a cure but it must be only on a national basis.

If there had been a national strike call instead of making a single club the scapegoat I would have refused to handle any match I had been given. I did a match at Millwall a fortnight ago. I went there with my eyes open after the attack on Norman Burtenshaw. I am not condoning what has happened at the Den. Don't think that.

I was punched on the face by a fan at Halifax a year ago. I wouldn't mind betting it was a damned sight harder blow than Norman got at Millwall. But his incident was bang in the spotlight and that is why people tend to regard this as Millwall business and not a national problem.

I disagreed with Howley. A ban at every ground would have been far too severe. It would have spoilt Saturday afternoons for three-quarters-of-a-million people, all but a handful of whom were innocent of any violence. We felt that by making a stand over one particular ground where a case had been proved, it would spur the authorities into taking remedial action at every ground.

The Football League were alarmed by our statement. They thought it should never have been issued. Alan Hardaker, the League secretary, issued one of his own later that day, trying to cool the situation. He said, however, that the League appreciated the feelings of the referees.

In talks with Mr Hardaker and Mr Len Shipman, Mr Lover was told that the League would ask Millwall to make alterations to their ground to ensure that fans were unable to jump on to the pitch in future. There was also a promise that the whole question of the safety of officials would be examined.

This was the assurance the referees' executive wanted. The

ban on Millwall matches was lifted. It would have been impossible to enforce, anyway. Six officials had volunteered to take Millwall's next home game, against Portsmouth, on 11 November, the day after the Association announced their boycott.

The referee was Dr Dennis Brady of Gloucester, who said it was like having his neck in a noose. If he turned down the appointment, he would be in trouble with the Football League. If he took it, the Association of Football League Referees and Linesmen would be unhappy. Like the rest of us, he was relieved when the League announced that they were going to tackle the encroachment problem, and our ban was lifted.

Mr Lover was also relieved. After he had appeared on TV to talk about the referees' case, his wife was phoned several times and told: 'If your husband doesn't lay off Millwall we're going to disfigure your pretty face.'

I wondered how the Millwall affair would affect my own career. I felt that it might ruin it. There were hundreds of referees queueing to get on to the League list.

The newspapers were full of headlines about Millwall's home match with Portsmouth and the end of 'the referees' revolt'. George Smith, the manager of Portsmouth, said the country was in a state of anarchy when such things happened. Mr Purser said he was sick and tired of the whole business and just wanted to see his team allowed to play some football.

Usually there are thirty police on duty at the Den for a normal Second Division match. But that number was doubled for the Portsmouth match. The crowd was 16,057, the largest of the season. At least Millwall ought to have been grateful for all the free publicity!

Police patrolled the pitch and Dr Brady was escorted on and off. As expected, there was no trouble. An announcer said over the loudspeaker: 'Don't go on to the pitch. Don't throw things after the match. Please go home quietly. The future of the club depends on you.'

One critic said Dr Brady was guarded as if he were General Moshe Dayan on a State visit to Cairo. Five policemen shepherded him out of the ground into a squad car outside. Another squad car travelled behind.

Millwall later made a report to the Football League claiming that referees were against them. That was a ludicrous suggestion. But I did feel sorry for them. What occurred at their ground could have happened anywhere. They were unlucky in that their incident came at a time when the referees were determined to take action.

Things improved after that. It became standard practice for police to escort officials from the pitch at all grounds. Chelsea built a fence at Stamford Bridge. UEFA, the European Football Association, laid down that no club could enter their competitions unless the fans were fenced off.

Since the Millwall affair, no referee has been attacked in England. So something was achieved! Some supporters never let me forget the Millwall business. There were chants of 'Millwall, Millwall' at other grounds when I made an unpopular decision. And I don't think Millwall themselves have forgiven me. Five years later, Millwall still claimed that referees were down on them.

6

Did Jackie Charlton score?

Sometimes a referee makes a decision which he knows is right but everyone else says is wrong. Such a decision was made by me at Elland Road, Leeds, on Monday, 26 April 1971, when I allowed a goal scored by the Leeds centre-half Jackie Charlton against Arsenal. I was the Cup Final referee.

It was the only goal of the match and it appeared to have sabotaged Arsenal's chances of winning the Double. Less than two weeks later, on 8 May, they were due to play Liverpool in the FA Cup Final at Wembley. 'Arsenal Robbed', said the newspaper headlines. For days I was pilloried. It worried me sick. I thought 'if the Arsenal players feel like that it is going to make the Cup Final a disaster'.

I was not down to referee the Leeds v Arsenal match. I was sitting at home on the Sunday afternoon when the telephone rang. George Readle asked if I would be available to make a switch. I was supposed to be taking the Colchester v Barrow match at Layer Road. That suited me fine. A local game. No controversy . . . I hoped!

Jim Finney, one of the best referees in the country, had been selected to handle the Leeds v Arsenal match but was hurt in a car crash. At ten o'clock on the Monday morning Mr Readle rang again and confirmed that I was going to Leeds. I packed my bag and left at eleven-thirty by car. If Arsenal won they would also win the League championship. Elland Road would be crammed. The atmosphere would be something special.

Thousands of Arsenal fans had travelled up the M1 for the match. Many of them couldn't get in. The police estimated that 20,000 supporters were locked out when the gates were closed before the kick-off. The tension was unbelievable.

During the long drive up I thought about what had happened in the Leeds v WBA match nine days before, when referee Ray Tinkler made a controversial decision. He decided that an Albion player was not interfering with play when in an offside position. Tinkler was assailed because it was said he had cost Leeds the game. Don Revie, the Leeds manager, was quoted as saying that Tinkler had ruined the season's work. Percy Woodward, the Leeds chairman, said it was about time they had professional referees. He said Tinkler would never referee at Leeds again.

The crowd came on the pitch and there were some nasty scenes before the police managed to clear them off. The FA ordered Leeds to play their first four matches of the following season away from home as a punishment and also fined the club £750. It was a classic case of a club blaming everything on the referee. The laws clearly state that all decisions are 'the opinion of the referee'. Only the referee can decide whether a player is interfering with play.

Ray Tinkler is known as 'Advantage' Tinkler in refereeing circles because he tends to give the advantage. He is a very able referee, one of the top men who is highly respected by his colleagues. He has never been afraid to give an unpopular decision. I thought Mr Revie's attack on him was quite uncalled-for and unnecessary. It contrasted with Revie's attitude after the Jackie Charlton goal against Arsenal.

The crowd at Elland Road on 26 April was 48,350, whereas the crowd at the match I was originally due to do, Colchester v Barrow, was 3,502. The noise was so great that it was difficult to hear what anyone was saying. I sweated profusely before the game simply because I was so tense. The players were even more tense.

More than ever before in my career, I had to get on top of this game from the start. I think I did. I thought it went well. Three players were booked, Terry Cooper for tripping George Graham, George Graham for belting Billy Bremner in the back, and Charlie George for kicking the ball away.

It was a tight hard game. There were 43 fouls, 22 against Arsenal and 21 against Leeds. I added on several minutes for injury and it was during this time that Charlton scored. He moved up to centre-forward. Allan Clarke passed to Bremner, Bremner to Charlton, and Charlton's shot went in off the post.

Arsenal skipper Frank McLintock stood with his arm raised appealing for offside. I was in a good position, level with the play. There was no doubt in my mind that an Arsenal player had put Charlton onside by his slowness in coming out. I looked at my linesman. He was in a good position too. His flag stayed down.

At half-time I had mentioned to my linesmen that one of the Arsenal players was slow coming out when the Arsenal defence moved up. That player was the left-back Bob McNab. And it was McNab who had now put Charlton onside.

I pointed to the centre and started to run upfield. Immediately I was set upon by a pack of Arsenal players. I had never seen players so incensed by one decision. They wanted me to consult the linesman. I refused. I pointed to the centre. The linesman had already indicated that he agreed with my decision. It didn't matter if he disagreed. It was my opinion that counted, not his.

There were so many players arguing and screaming around me that it was impossible to move or try to restart the game. It was the kind of situation where I might have had to book all of them, or abandon the match. I could understand their frustration. But there was no going back. I had made my decision and was sticking to it.

Luckily Charlie George inadvertently broke the tension. He picked up the ball and kicked it into the stand. I promptly booked him for ungentlemanly conduct. That broke up the demonstration. The sight of the book coming out cooled tempers.

Police cleared away supporters who had started to come to the side of the pitch, and Bertie Mee did his best to get the Arsenal players to play again. Eventually the game was restarted and went on for several more minutes before I blew for the last time.

The Arsenal players were still expressing their anger as they came off. I remember goalkeeper Bob Wilson saying that it was never a goal, though how he could tell in his position I didn't know.

Charlton said there was an Arsenal player back on the line when he shot, and the ball went in off the back of his leg. It was McNab, he said.

McLintock thought Charlton was five yards offside. Don Howe, then Arsenal's coach, said: 'The goal was well offside and should not have been allowed, but we have to take the bad things with the good. Referees are only human and they make mistakes from time to time.'

Howe was sitting on the halfway line, not the best position from which to judge. Revie, sitting near him, diplomatically said that he didn't see the incident.

Offside is one of the trickiest decisions for a referee in modern football. Most teams use offside as a tactic. When they get the ball someone shouts 'out' and the defenders rush up-field. I am sure many people who regularly attend football do not understand the offside law.

It is the time the ball was last played that counts in deciding whether a forward ball is offside, not where the forward is standing when he receives the ball. A player like Don Rogers of Crystal Palace is so quick that he can be yards ahead of the last defender when he receives the ball but still be onside. Jimmy Greaves was another player who made life difficult for the referee and linesmen.

Jackie Charlton didn't come into this category because he is not a fast mover. The dispute over his goal arose because of a defender's mistake which at the time was detected only by the officials.

Our dressing-room after that match was not a happy place. I believed we had not put a foot wrong in the ninety minutes. I thought about the Cup Final and how it would affect me. One of the teams would be prejudiced against me. That was no way to handle the biggest match of one's career. Leeds must have thought they had got something for nothing.

It was a bad period for me. I wanted to talk to someone but couldn't. I had to live with it. When I got home my wife said the incident had been shown on TV. 'I don't care how many times they show it, it was still a good goal,' I said. The inevitable telephone calls started. They were going to get me. I wouldn't reach Wembley alive.

I had refused to speak to the Press after the match but the pressure was so great the next day that I had to say something. The sporting nation seemed to assume that the Arsenal players were right and I was wrong.

I told one correspondent: 'In my honest opinion Jack Charlton was onside when he scored. The linesman agreed that it was a good goal and did not flag.

'It would have been the easiest thing in the world to disallow that sort of late goal in a match so full of tension. But once you start doing that sort of thing you might as well pack up. You must do what you believe to be right. I say again, it was a good goal and I would make the same decision again.

'This will not affect my handling of the Cup Final between Arsenal and Liverpool on Saturday week. Referees do not allow things to overlap from one game to another.'

The important word in that statement was 'honest'. I made what I thought was an honest decision. The next day Bertie Mee was asked whether he would request the FA to replace me as the Cup Final referee.

'Certainly not', he said.

I never even considered such a move. I thought the referee had a very good game until he made what I thought was a wrong decision.

He was admirable in handling a game which would have been extremely difficult for any referee. Mr Burtenshaw has been in charge of two other Arsenal games this season and on each occasion I went to compliment him upon his handling of those games.

I have several duties and the major one is to maintain the dignity and reputation of Arsenal Football Club. I would like to make it clear that I did not attempt to go on to the field or speak to the referee after the decisive goal had been awarded. I went down to calm my players and tell them to get on with the game.

I cannot criticize them for what they did. After all they too, like referees, are human beings. I felt for the boys who had slogged out so endlessly, and for the young players in particular it was a bitter pill to swallow.

I accept what they did. It was a human reaction. Let us say we lost a battle but not a war. It will be great to win the title at Tottenham in our last match on the Monday before the Final.

That is precisely what Arsenal did. By Cup Final Saturday, they had no reason to be still angry about Charlton's goal.

Later in the week the Arsenal players went to their usual hotel just outside Bournemouth to relax – 'to let the tension drain away,' said McNab. By then they had had a chance to see the TV film of the Charlton incident several times. Now they began to accept that perhaps I was right after all. McNab's statement was the most damning evidence:

Charlton might have been onside after all. One or two of our lads who have seen it again on TV think he was.

I know it was much closer than a lot of people seemed to think when it happened. But we are happy that it is this way.

It no longer seems important. It is no longer hanging over us that we were robbed. It becomes a small incident soon forgotten.

I only wished someone had said that at the time! I was known as the referee who robbed Arsenal of the title at Leeds. The correction never receives as much prominence as the original charge!

I was heartened to hear that Arsenal were going to invite me to their Cup Final banquet. The club chairman, Denis Hill-Wood, said: 'We have no ill feeling towards him. If the decision had cost us the championship – and we haven't lost it yet – we would still have invited him. After all, he didn't do it on purpose, and all the players thought he generally had a blinder at Leeds.'

The *Sun* cartoonist Rigby had a cartoon of a referee dressed in armour and carrying whips and a ball and chain. One of the players was imploring him to come out on to the field. 'Aw, come on ref,' the player was saying. 'Maybe you won't have to give an offside decision today!'

7

You're bent!

Towards the end of the 1970–1 season I was in the referees' dressing-room, at one of the lesser-known grounds, beginning to work up some tension. When you are at Anfield or Old Trafford the nervous excitement which makes you perform better comes easier. Sometimes it is hard to get yourself into this state at a Fourth Division match.

I bounced the ball up and down agitatedly. A director came in. 'Congratulations,' he said.

'What for?' I asked.

'Haven't they told you?'

'Told me what?'

'You've got the Cup Final!'

I was staggered. I wasn't even an international referee. The season before I had been taken off the FIFA list. The director thought I should have known that I had been picked to handle the FA Cup. But no one had told me officially.

It was ten to three. The teams were due to kick off in ten minutes' time. I was in a terrible state. I do not know how I got through that match.

Being chosen to referee the FA Cup Final is the highest accolade any referee can receive. It means they think you are the best. In previous years the FA Cup Final used to be given to the senior man on the list who was about to retire. It was a reward for services rendered. But the Football Association realized that this might not have been the correct way to go about things. The change came after Eric Jennings of

Stourbridge refereed the Chelsea v Leeds Cup Final in 1970. The general verdict was that Jennings did not have a good match. It was not an easy game to handle. Some of the players on either side disliked each other and it showed.

I was so excited after hearing about the Cup Final that I decided to buy a bottle of champagne and take it home to celebrate with my wife Dorothy. But the Norwich train broke down and I had to sit on the news for an hour and a half at Ipswich. It was eleven-thirty when I eventually arrived home by car from Norwich.

'I've got the Cup Final!' I said to Dorothy. She broke down and cried. The only other people I told were my children and parents. No one else knew. The information might not have been correct. The Director might have got it wrong.

Three weeks later the telephone rang and a man from the Football Association said, 'How would you like to referee the Cup Final?' So many days had elapsed that I began to think I wasn't going to referee it after all, so it was still something of a surprise to hear the confirmation.

'Don't pull my leg,' I said.

'No, it's true,' the official replied. There was a silence.

'Are you still there?'

'Yes,' I said. 'It's fantastic.'

The official replied: 'Don't disclose the information until Monday after the announcement. We don't want it to leak out.'

Two days later I went on a long trip with some other referees to a meeting of our association. We discussed who might get the Cup Final. One or two of them thought I had a chance. When they asked me, I mentioned the name of another referee.

The next Monday the news was released and the phone was constantly engaged. Takings in my shop jumped to £60. Kit manufacturers rang with offers of a new outfit. Every Cup Final official wears a new outfit but he always wears old boots. A Cup Final is no place to try out new boots. The BBC came down to film me running along the beach. I was something of a celebrity.

The finalists were Arsenal and Liverpool. Some critics thought it might be a crunch match, but it couldn't have been as bad as Chelsea v Leeds the year before.

For three weeks I played that game over in my mind every

night. The build up in tension was incredible. I trained hard – I always do – and knew that I would be fit enough to cope. But what if there were some really nasty incidents? That is what a referee fears most at a big match. No one had ever been sent off at Wembley. Would I be the first referee to order a player off?

The night before I was the guest of honour at the Lonsar rally of referees at St Pancras town hall. Two thousand or more referees from all over the country come every year to attend this function. We have our own five-a-side tournament. The spotlight plays on you. You feel as though you have made it at last. But always at the back of your mind is the thought about tomorrow's game – what if there is a big controversy? I had been involved in plenty of incidents in my career. I never sought controversy but it seemed to follow me around.

I went to bed at eleven but didn't sleep well. Officially the players taking part in the Final are allowed twelve tickets each. The referee gets two free ones and is allowed to buy four from the FA to make sure relatives can see the match.

At nine-thirty we left to walk from the Great Western Hotel to the Football Association.

At the FA the referee selects the match ball. There are thirty balls laid out in a small room. None of them bears the manufacturer's name. Ten are yellow, ten red and ten white. I do not know why the yellow and red ones are there, because invariably a white ball is selected. The balls are numbered and the referee picks out three.

I was uncertain about one point. Was the Cup Final referee supposed to talk to the players in the dressing-room before the match? I asked to speak to the FA secretary, Denis Follows, to clarify this.

Mr Follows did not seem too pleased to see me. 'Everyone wants to see me without an appointment today,' he said. I apologized for troubling him. 'Well, if you feel it is necessary to go into the dressing-rooms, you can,' he said.

The officials got into a Rolls-Royce – myself, the two linesmen and a reserve linesman who always changes in case something happens to the three chosen officials.

The traffic builds up around Wembley even when there are more than three hours before the kick-off. The fans standing outside the stadium peer through the windows to see which big nob is arriving. You may well feel important but you know they have come to see the players, not you. The referee is anonymous. One fan put his head through the window and said, 'I suppose you only come to one fucking match a year!'

We had lunch in the stadium restaurant – fish. I did not feel like eating much. We walked round the pitch to see it was marked out right!

The officials' dressing-room at Wembley is a pretty pawky place. There is not much room for four men to change. There is no bath, just one shower which by tradition the referee uses first. It is a plain brick room and the toilet has a half-door. Some contrast to the Royal loo which we had a look at on our conducted tour round the stadium.

Dicky Bird, the FA official who looks after the referees, is in the room to answer any queries. He is the man in the long black overcoat who is seen leading the procession out of the tunnel.

Lying on the table in the middle of the room is a small brown parcel for each official – a pair of laces and a jockstrap each from the Football Association.

When I came off the pitch to change, Sam Leitch of the BBC asked me for an interview. I had not been interviewed on national TV before. The Football League did not encourage it. My first reaction, I admit, may appear to have been rather mercenary. 'How much?' I said.

He looked a bit surprised. 'We'll give you something,' he said. I know that may have sounded bad on my part but remember that the players under me that day would probably pick up £1,000 a man from their perks pool. They were no doubt receiving the same amount again for appearing in the Cup Final. My reward was fifteen guineas and a medal. Not long before, it was a fee *or* a medal. Everyone chose the gold medal.

By the time I had paid my children's expenses and for their tickets, I was running a loss. All I had to show for my work which was being seen by 250 million people around the world was a gold medal. Yet I looked on myself as a professional the way the players did. And how many times in your career do you do a Cup Final? No one has ever done one twice. Two months later I received a cheque for £20 from the BBC for that interview. It was not a good interview. I was in no mental condition to say very much that made sense.

Not much was spoken in our dressing-room. The toilet, like the ones in the players' dressing-rooms, was in continual use.

Two-twenty. Time to go into the players' rooms to give them a brief talk. I was apprehensive about going into the Arsenal room. As I have already written, I had angered their players two weeks earlier by allowing a Jackie Charlton goal at Leeds which they thought was offside. I was thinking about this as the attendant swung back the heavy, iron door. Bertie Mee had been quoted as saying he had no recriminations about that decision. 'Mr Burtenshaw is a very good referee,' he had said. Mee was not in the dressing-room when I entered. I saw Frank McLintock. He had been particularly angry at Leeds. But my decision had not stopped them winning the League championship.

I held my hand out. 'Congratulations on winning the title,' I said. He took my hand but he didn't say a word. He didn't want to know. Christ, I thought, he's still got that Charlton goal on his mind.

Bob Wilson, the goalkeeper, was more affable. I said just one thing to the players: 'I want to emphasize that the laws of the game are applicable here as they are in any other game. I say that because I feel some players don't think that is the case.' That was all I said.

As I left, Bertie Mee came in. 'Pleased to see you, Norman,' he said. 'I hope everything goes well for you and you have a good game.'

That made me feel better. I have always had the highest regard for Bertie Mee. I never saw him go off in a rage, not even that night at Elland Road.

Bill Shankly looked strained in the Liverpool dressing-room but he too had time to be friendly. 'I hope you have a good game,' he said. He is another manager I respect.

Back in the referee's room the telegrams were laid out. There were thirty-eight for me, some from people I never knew. One was from the former Charlton player Sailor Brown. Except for refereeing one of his matches in my early days, I

68

hadn't met him for some years. He told me then: 'You'll go a long way.'

The tension was acute now. Suddenly the bell jangled – the signal for the teams and officials to line up outside in the tunnel.

Two-forty-eight. This is the time the tension really grips you. Inside the dressing-room there is silence. The chants and roars of the crowd are not heard. But in that tunnel the noise hits you. Everyone is going to look at me, you imagine to yourself. Of course they won't. They will only look at you if you make a mistake. Mistakes! What if I miss something in the first minute?

There are some hard men in these sides. Peter Storey is playing for Arsenal. Tommy Smith for Liverpool. But Arsenal and Liverpool are not dirty sides. Everything will be fine. No need to worry.

The players jog about in their track suits. Their studs get roughed up! No one says anything. Faces looked drained. The TV cameras intrude.

The procession starts to move forward. 'Don't look at the crowd,' I keep telling myself. 'Don't take any notice of them. Concentrate on the game.'

We lined up in front of the Royal Box. Prince Philip shook me by the hand. 'Where do you come from?' he asked.

'Great Yarmouth,' I replied.

'I was down there recently,' he said. I was struck by his pleasant, calm nature. If it was possible to put anyone at ease in a situation like this, he had done it.

Three o'clock. The first whistle. The game was away! Soon Storey brought down Steve Heighway and I blew for a free kick. I didn't speak to Storey. Later, as the Liverpool goal-keeper Ray Clemence came out to the edge of the area to collect an overhit pass up the middle, Storey charged into him, knocking him over.

It was a grossly uncalled-for challenge. Storey had no chance of getting to the ball first. The Liverpool defenders went beserk. Trouble!

Tommy Smith shouted, 'He's fouled again. He's done it again.' Nothing annoys footballers more than a foul on the goalkeeper. Outfield players can kick each other and sometimes not too much is said, but immediately the goalkeeper is felled coming out for the ball, bedlam breaks loose.

It was an offence that warranted a caution and I would have cautioned Storey. But Smith was making so much noise that I had to speak to him first.

'I'll deal with it,' I said as calmly as I could. 'Leave it to me.' I never believe in rushing into any scene. If I appear flustered that will only make the situation worse.

By this time Storey was getting out of range. I would have to call him back if I wanted to caution him. I warned him later. I think he knew enough about me to realize that next time he could be in serious trouble.

Everything went well after that. It was a clean game between two tight, hard-working sides. Near half-time I gave an indirect free-kick against Peter Simpson for obstructing Alun Evans just inside the penalty area. Arsenal's wall lined up and Ian Callaghan tapped the ball sideways for the left-back Alec Lindsay to hit just inside the far post. Wilson made a good save, scrambling it round the post.

I blew for half-time as the corner kick came over. I was standing by the far post. I turned to look towards my linesmen. McLintock suddenly ran across behind the goal and came up to me and said, 'You're bent.'

That was all he said. I was astounded. No one had ever accused me of being bent. What a time and place! It was an astonishing thing to say. I wondered what brought it on. Was it the free kick seconds earlier? Or the memory of the Charlton goal at Leeds?

I never spoke. I thought I had done a fair job in the first half. I had kept up with the play, taken up good positions and read the game well. The crowd had not booed or jeered me, at least!

Back in the dressing-room I told my linesmen what McLintock had said. 'I'm not going to let it worry me,' I said. But I did think of it as we walked up the tunnel for the second half. Was it the big bonuses which made players – nice, ordinary fellows off the field – say things like that? Were the pressures sometimes too much for them?

Later I met McLintock at a Rothman's lunch. We were both

surrounded by people. 'This is the only player who ever told me I was bent,' I said. McLintock laughed.

It was a very hot, sunny day that Cup Final Saturday in May. I had covered a lot of ground in the first half and had sweated a lot. At half-time I felt absolutely shattered. In terms of distance, a referee runs farther than any of the players. I drank several cups of tea and stuffed some glucose tablets into me.

The second half flowed pretty well. Neither side wanted to come out. There were few goal-scoring chances. I kept thinking, 'I wish someone would score. We don't want extra time.'

But there was extra time. Some of the players had their socks down at the end of ninety minutes. Strangely, I felt more relaxed at the end of ninety minutes than I was at half-time. The game had gone well. I thought I had done a good job.

In the brief break before the start of extra time the players came to the side of the pitch for drinks, consolation and advice. Bertie Mee thrust a bottle at me. 'Here's some lemonade,' he said. I thought that said a lot for the man. This was a vital moment. Each second was vital but he could still find time for the referee. Bill Shankly, too, came over. 'You okay?' he asked.

I said I was. In fact, looking at some of the players, I thought I was in better condition for the next thirty minutes than they were.

Liverpool scored first. Peter Thompson, their substitute, passed to Steve Heighway on the left and for once Arsenal's defence was undermanned. Heighway streaked off down the left side of the pitch with what was left of the Arsenal defence trying to push him wide.

Heighway's unorthodoxy really got him that goal. Goalkeeper Bob Wilson expected him to pull the ball back as he swept in towards the by-line. Wilson came off his post a yard for this eventuality. Heighway had so much room that he could have gone on. But he shot, much too soon, I thought, and the ball went behind Wilson on the near post into the far corner of the net. I said to myself, 'Why couldn't he do that in the ninety minutes?'

My first reaction when a goal is scored is to turn and run

back to the centre circle. I do that because if I stand around there could be trouble from players appealing for all kinds of things. In some matches there is nothing to appeal about, but players will still complain and raise their voices. I never note down that a goal has been scored. The only entries I make on my card are the names of players I have cautioned. It is no use asking me the score of a game. I never keep it!

Soon Arsenal were level at 1–1. It was a messy goal. Eddie Kelly, substituting for the injured Storey, challenged Emlyn Hughes and Tommy Smith to a bouncing ball in the penalty area. Kelly got there first, and as his half-hit shot went towards the corner of the net George Graham seemed to get a touch to put it in. Well, that was what everyone thought at the time, but the TV playbacks showed that George Graham didn't touch the ball. It was Kelly's goal.

It makes no difference to me who scores a goal. I don't record goalscorers. Stalemate again. I hoped someone would score a winner. The referee likes to get his medal at Wembley, not at a replay on some routine First Division ground which he has visited many times before.

Players were going down with cramp all around me; even Emlyn Hughes, one of the fittest players I ever knew. I felt fine myself. Those hours of running on the sands had made me fitter than I had ever been in my career.

When Charlie George shot the winning goal I felt like joining in the celebrations, not because it was Arsenal winning but because one side was leading and there would now be a result. I blew my whistle for the last time in that match and knelt down on the ground as though in prayer.

It was a reaction from the mental tension. I had prepared for the physical stress but had under-estimated what this game would take out of me mentally. I was mentally exhausted. The effort of concentrating every second of 120 minutes on the play – ignoring the crowd – had drained me.

Suddenly I thought, 'what the hell are you kneeling down for?' So I got up and embraced one of my linesmen, Gordon Kew. Players embrace each other on such an occasion as this, so why not officials? I think he felt the same relief as I did – that there had not been one real controversy in the 120 minutes.

As we waited at the bottom of the steps that lead to the Royal

Box for the players to receive their medals, I saw Bill Shankly standing there. He looked full up.

'Very good game,' I said. He didn't reply. He was a lonely man at that moment. I received my medal and grasped it hard. There was an empty feeling. Everything now was an anticlimax. The players and officials were supposed to line up for the playing of *God Save the Queen*, but it was a shambles.

Several people congratulated me on the game and said that it had gone well. Denis Howell, the former Labour Minister of Sport, and Sir Stanley Rous, both ex-referees themselves, said they thought I had done a good job. But the tribute that gave me most satisfaction came from Mr McMullen, chairman of the Referees Committee.

That night the officials went to both banquets. Arsenal's was complete confusion. It was impossible to speak to anyone. But at Liverpool's, the tone was quiet and there was no gaiety.

Bill Shankly called us over to his table. 'Well done,' he said. 'Glad you came in. Do you know, I think you were right about that Charlton goal at Leeds.'

Altogether I made five appearances as an official at Wembley. That fact may not be in the *Guinness Book of Records* but it is a record all the same. My first appearance was as a linesman in the 1964–5 Cup Final between Leeds and Liverpool. That was the game which was called the most boring FA Cup Final ever played at Wembley. Liverpool won 2–1 after extra time. It was a hard, tight game and neither side took any chances.

Leeds were beginning to make a name for themselves at that time. They were a hard side. But except for one bad foul by Johnny Giles there were few incidents and the game went off quietly for the referee, Bill Clements, and his two linesmen. Bill Clements lectured Giles, whereas if the same foul had taken place five years later, he would have cautioned him.

In those days it was unthinkable to book a player at Wembley. I never knew why. A foul at Wembley should be the same as a foul anywhere else. The laws of the game were the same whatever the venue or however important the occasion. This tradition of not cautioning players at Wembley

73

disappeared in the late sixties. No player has been sent off in a Cup Final, and I think that could change too.

I was not aware that it was a boring game. I was so absorbed in my task that when we came in at the end I said, 'What a great game.' Perhaps I meant occasion, not game.

I was probably the most anonymous person at Wembley that day. No one notices the linesman until he makes a mistake or a decision that half the crowd do not agree with. There was one offside which riled some supporters, otherwise I was right out of the limelight, which was how I preferred it.

I was the referee on my next visit to Wembley – the 1965–6 Amateur Cup Final in which Wealdstone beat Hendon 3–1. This was a far better match for the spectators. There were 45,000 fans there that day, and though the atmosphere was nothing like that at a FA Cup Final, it was a memorable occasion for me.

Almost a year after the Arsenal v Liverpool FA Cup Final I was given the Chelsea v Stoke League Cup Final. This was a difficult game for any referee because the League's clean-up campaign had started, and officials were anxious to see that their showpiece game at Wembley was controlled in the spirit of their memorandum.

No referee thinks to himself: 'I've got X out there today, he's given me trouble in the past. I'll have to watch out for him.' He likes to treat each player the same and to forget about what happened in the past.

There were some awkward customers in the Chelsea and Stoke sides that day. Peter Osgood and Ron Harris in the Chelsea side, Denis Smith, an aggressive centre-half, in the Stoke side. Osgood v Smith might well be an explosive encounter. It was. In the early minutes Osgood clipped Jimmy Greenhoff from the side and knocked him down.

I was so close to the incident that I made a mistake in not booking Osgood right then. I was half-a-yard away. If I had been several yards away I could have judged Osgood's intentions better. Greenhoff and the other Stoke players were incensed.

'He's an animal,' said one. Osgood didn't say much. He never does when he knows he is in the wrong. Greenhoff was treated and resumed the game with his arm hanging limp.

The first half-hour was the trickiest period I had experienced at Wembley. There was plenty of nastiness from both sides and I think my mistake with Osgood was partly responsible. If I had cautioned him, the other players might not have behaved the way they did. Eventually I did caution Osgood for treading on Smith. Osgood asked me what it was for. 'Ungentlemanly conduct,' I said. 'You could have avoided him but you walked on him.'

I booked two Stoke players, Alan Bloor and Mike Pejic, both for bringing Chris Garland down when in a good position. In the game these fouls are called 'professional fouls'. Personally, I think they are despicable.

Garland was through on each occasion and could easily have scored. If he had, Chelsea, not Stoke, would have won the League Cup. So perhaps Bloor and Pejic were justified in their own minds. I could never justify such conduct.

As I left the field I touched the goalpost as a sentimental gesture. I thought that would be the last time I would ever referee a game at Wembley. But there was to be a fifth occasion – the Three v Six Common Market Celebration game on 3 January 1973, the game to hail Britain's entry into the Common Market.

The Press underplayed this game but it was a great honour for me to be asked to handle it. Some of the world's greatest players took part – Gunter Netzer, Gerd Muller, Franz Beckenbauer and Bobby Moore. Ken Sweet, one of the linesmen, did not arrive until four-thirty on the day of the match. The other linesman from Scotland was also held up because of fog. The Six players came into London in dribs and drabs, some even as late as the day of the match.

A hire-car was to take us from the FA to Wembley. The driver did not know the route and a journey which normally took half-an-hour lasted an hour-and-a-half. Reg Paine, the FA official in charge of referees, was frantic. It was not the best preparation for a big match which was being televised halfway round Europe.

I picked out three balls costing £15 apiece from which the ball to be used would be chosen. A foreign gentleman came into the referee's room before the start, holding a black and yellow spotted ball.

'Here is the ball we will be using,' he said. I told him that the ball had already been chosen – a white one.

Helmut Schoen, the manager of the Six team, then intervened. 'This is the ball we want to use,' he said, pointing to the black and yellow one. We had never used a ball like that in a big match in England and I did not intend to start now.

I referred Herr Schoen to the Football Association. He came back to say that after joint discussion it was confirmed that a white ball would be used. White balls seem to show up better on TV than coloured ones. There was an ironic twist to this story. The white ball which was used went out of shape by the end of the game!

It was more like an exhibition match than a serious game of football. There were hardly any tackles and the build-ups were slow and deliberate. But there was a surfeit of skill from the Continental players and I am sure the crowd enjoyed watching it.

I had to abandon my usual style of refereeing. I found I was getting out of position by anticipating the game to flow in the way of a normal international match. I had to slow down!

Peter Lorimer complained on a couple of occasions about not being given corners but otherwise there was no dissent. It was a pleasure to referee such a match.

There was another mix-up, however, this time about the use of substitutes. Before the match someone from the BBC asked me how many substitutes were allowed. I said two. An official from the FA agreed. But when the teams came up the tunnel for the second half I noticed more than two new faces in the Six team.

'How many substitutes have you got in your side?' I asked Netzer, who speaks quite good English.

'Four,' he said. I couldn't do much about it. I could hardly order two of them back into the dressing-room. So I took the common-sense way out and let them get on with it.

The Duke of Kent presented me with a silver rose bowl worth £50 after the match, and I still have that out-of-shape ball.

8

The night the refs got their books out

17 August 1971 was the night the referees got their books out and started booking players. Thirty-two players were cautioned in fifteen matches.

The players didn't know what hit them. Noel Cantwell, the Coventry manager, said, 'The game is going mad and I don't know why.'

Derek Dougan, chairman of the Professional Footballers Association, said, 'If this continues we will have eighty-five minutes of stoppages and five minutes of football. It seems that there is no longer any room in the game for physical contact.'

The newspaper critics reacted just as indignantly. The referees were killing the game, they all said. This nonsense of booking players for the most trivial things had got to stop. The newspapers called it 'the refs' revolution' and 'the clampdown'. No one had a good word for it.

Even a level-headed manager like Bill Nicholson was aghast. 'It is time we were told what was going on,' he said. 'It seems the Football League are giving the referees books and pencils and trying to get them to frighten the players.'

The first impact of the so-called refs' revolution was felt at Portman Road, Ipswich, where Tonbridge referee Ron Challis cautioned six players in the match in which Ipswich beat

Coventry 3–1. One of the players was cautioned for deliberate hand ball on the halfway line.

The Ipswich manager Bobby Robson was just as incensed as Noel Cantwell. 'The game won't continue if they keep booking people like this,' he said.

The next night seven players were cautioned in the Tottenham v Newcastle 0–0 draw at White Hart Lane. Altogether thirty-eight players were booked that Wednesday night and three were sent off. One of the players sent off was George Best, at Stamford Bridge. I was the referee who sent him off.

In the first eleven weeks of the so-called revolution a total of seven hundred players were cautioned. By 15 December the total had risen to one thousand. The five-strong staff at the disciplinary department at the FA offices in Lancaster Gate had to work late coping with the rush.

'We will work through the night if necessary to get through all the appeals,' said Vernon Stokes, chairman of the Disciplinary Committee. As the weeks went by, the players' anger hardly abated. They thought the referees were ruining the game, their game. The amateurs were at it again. And the gulf between the players and referees grew wider. Referees were more despised than ever.

Bobby Moncur, the Newcastle captain, summed it up when he said of that game at White Hart Lane: 'We will be going out there with handbags soon. The referees are turning it into a game for cissies.'

Why was it thought necessary to clamp down on the players? Whose idea was it? And why didn't they tell the players first? Many people thought it was a badly organized bungle, and that impression still lingered on two years afterwards.

When I first came on to the League list, players did not kick each other from behind. When the ball was played to the centre-forward he was allowed to turn with it. Then, without anyone realizing it was happening, the centre-half started to pressure the centre-forward. Soon, the centre-half was sliding into the back of him. The tackle from behind became standard practice. Hardly a centre-forward in the land survived the season without some kind of injury to his Achilles tendon or ankle.

Players like Geoff Hurst and Rodney Marsh would complain about this, but except for blowing for a foul, referees did not do much about it. One of the chief sufferers was George Best, who ironically became one of the first players to be sent off when the clean-up started.

In the early sixties it was rare for a defender to bring an opponent down from behind when it looked as though the other player would score a goal. By the end of the decade it was common practice.

The professional foul was developed. Defenders were expected to chop opponents down as a rehearsed tactic. If they were standing on the goal line and the goalkeeper was beaten and the ball was about to cross the line, they were expected to fist the ball away and concede a penalty. The guy might miss it. His team wouldn't score after all. All this reduced the number of goals and cut down the entertainment of the paying customers, but no one worried much about that. The object was to avoid giving away goals, to stop the other side winning and to make sure that your side won something.

The philosophy that overtook football in England was simple: win at all costs. If two players were chasing the same ball the possibility was that one would be trying to hold the other off with his arm and the latter would be pulling the first player's shirt. Certain clubs instructed players to stand in front of the goalkeeper to put him off. Always a player was told to stand on the ball to slow down the taking of a free kick.

At throw-ins, we had a player jumping up and down in front of the thrower to distract him. This, of course, was an act of ungentlemanly conduct. The managers and coaches condoned all this because they said football was becoming more professional. They failed to realize what they were doing to the game.

Of course not every player was like this. Most of the matches I controlled in the Third and Fourth Divisions were honest. There were tackles from behind, but most of the fouls were not malicious.

Most of the Second Division teams, too, were pretty straightforward. The nice managers like Jimmy Adamson and Gordon Jago made their teams play the right way.

But up at the top, the pressures were forcing players to do

things which were deceitful and nasty. The games I hated refereeing were those involving the top four clubs in the Second Division. Often these would be kicking matches. Coaches said openly that you had to kick your way out of the Second Division, and some sides did. The reason they did this was money; their gates would be more than double in the First Division and the players would be on higher wages with the prospect of bigger bonuses if they won matches.

In the early sixties I do not remember much viciousness in the matches I controlled. The foul off the ball was rare. Players didn't argue much. Slowly it all changed and the referees were nearly as much to blame as the players and the managers and the coaches because they should have spotted it and done something about it themselves.

But it was hard for them to act because a lot of people claimed that it was possible to tackle from behind. One referee couldn't act on his own because if he did his marks would fall off and he would find himself out of a job. The quickest way to go down the scale is to become known as a book-happy referee. The clubs don't like you any more.

I used to shudder when I saw big fellows like Duncan Forbes, the Norwich centre-half, go into tackles from behind. Most central defenders were at it. Bobby Bell when he was at Ipswich; Derek Jefferson, Ipswich and later Wolves; John McGrath of Southampton; John Roberts, Arsenal and later Birmingham; Denis Smith of Stoke. One of the worst I saw was Terry Branston of Northampton.

You couldn't blame them. They were doing their job. Once I saw John O'Hare, the Derby centre-forward, a big, broad-chested fellow, completely flattened by McGrath. Was this what the game is all about, I thought?

But there were some players who held off; for instance, Jackie Charlton of Leeds. And there were others, such as Terry Cooper, Charlton's team mate, and Peter Rodrigues of Sheffield Wednesday, who could tackle from the side and pluck the ball away without first touching the player's legs. But too often tackles were on man and ball.

The ugliness that crept into football came, I believe, from our extended participation in European competitions. There was more to play for now. The winners of the League Cup qualified for the Fairs Cup, as it was then, or UEFA Cup as it is now. So the League Cup Final was no longer a showpiece game. It had to be played hard. No prisoners had to be taken. So for the first time, players began to be cautioned at Wembley.

The FA Cup Final itself suffered. The winners went into the European Cup Winners Cup and could earn £100,000 or more. Cup Finals, traditionally entertaining and open matches, started to get tight. The tackling grew wilder. The Wembley pitch seemed to get smaller.

The top clubs in the First Divison qualified for the UEFA Cup. In the old days of the Fairs Cup, clubs were invited because they came from a city that had a trade fair. The Fairs Cup was something of a social occasion. It had its troubles like all competitions against foreign opponents, but clubs were unable to make their fortune from it so the players treated it as a holiday.

Now for a club like Manchester United or Spurs to be out of Europe was something of a financial disaster. The pressure was there every season to win something. Coming seventh or eighth in the First Division and playing some attractive football which the fans liked to see was no longer good enough.

There was one strident sound echoing right the way through football: the ting-a-ling of the cash-register. The players were caught up in it too. If they found themselves out of the first team their wage might be halved. So they did what they were told. If the coach said 'take that man out', they took him out.

The players were leading new, expansive lives. They owned £20,000 houses, had two cars, and some sent their children to private schools. Football was a way of getting into a new social stratum. None of them wanted to give all that up, so they conformed.

I did not believe that any of them thought about the money while they were on the field. No player missed a penalty and said, 'Christ, that's £50 down the drain.' But the tension of having to succeed was always with them, before the game, during the game when they were absorbed in the struggle and not thinking about the wage-packet, and afterwards when it was time to go home.

It was getting harder and harder to referee matches. There were more arguments. Players appealed for everything. You never saw anyone laughing any more. The Football League knew that something was wrong and wanted to change it. The players were reluctant to change. They said the hatchet men had to be stopped, but seemed unwilling to do anything about it themselves. The managers could have stopped the hatchet men but they didn't.

Referees were loath to caution players when they knew it was necessary. One referee who never liked cautioning players was Geoff Roper of Stowmarket. He believed in talking to them nicely and lecturing them. He was a good referee but he upset one or two managers. Once he delayed the start of a game at Chelsea because the two teams were wearing stockings which clashed. He asked the Chelsea players to change.

I was appearing on a TV programme once when I met Alec Stock, now the Fulham manager. We were talking about Geoff Roper, who had then been removed from the League list.

'He had to go,' said Mr Stock.

'Why had he got to go?' I asked. 'What did he do wrong?'

But that was the way managers thought. What Mr Stock did not know was that Geoff Roper's ten-year-old son suddenly started to go blind at that time and he was under acute mental strain.

In the summer of 1971 the referees talked about the foul tackle from behind and the attendant ills of the modern game. George Readle, the Football League official then in charge of the referees, sought our opinions. It was at this time that the League decided to clean the game up. They held a meeting with the FA whose views were similar. The League sent out a memorandum to every referee and linesman. The tackle from behind was to be banned. Any player who committed it was in future to be cautioned. Later he was to be docked four points in the new disciplinary system. The player who handled deliberately to stop another player gaining a definite advantage or scoring would also be booked. So would the persistent arguer. The message in the memorandum was to administer the laws of the game as they should be administered. I think the League felt we had been too lenient. It was a view I shared myself.

The saddest part of the story of the clean-up was that the referees had to be told. It would have been better had we initiated the campaign ourselves. But we all knew that there would be no chance of this happening unless the League gave us their backing.

At the same time as the League were acting, the FA sent letters to every club in the country reminding them about what constituted fair and unfair play. Clubs were asked to pin these notices on dressing-room doors. Most did, but a few refused to co-operate.

On Sunday, 15 August 1971, referees gathered at meetings all over the country to be briefed on their new responsibilities. Reg Leafe, one of the most respected former referees, took the meeting I attended in London. It was a very satisfactory meeting. Reg said the things I believed in myself. We were being given licence to do our jobs properly. The referee who cautioned several players in a match would be supported.

Tuesday, 17 August, saw the start of the campaign. The reactions from within and outside the game were hysterical. Apparently those managers who had been pleading for years for the ball players to be given a chance didn't really mean it if it meant one of their own players being cautioned.

The main objection was that no one had been warned first. The players had no notification in advance. Cliff Lloyd, the secretary of the PFA, said this was quite wrong. In my view, it was quite right. Contrary to popular opinion, I thought the League's handling of the clean-up campaign was brilliant. If the League had called a big meeting and told the players and the managers there would have been a huge outcry (as indeed there was afterwards). The opposition would have been so great that I doubt whether the campaign would have got off the ground. The players might have called a token strike!

But after being hit hard with the book in the first few days, the players began to realize what they could and could no longer do on the football field. There were mistaken interpretations of the memorandum by referees, which was inevitable. You cannot brief eighty-three men and expect them all to carry out the briefing to the last precise details.

At White Hart Lane, for example, Lowestoft referee Ray Johnston booked a player for hand ball near the trainers' bench when the ball was going out of play. Some people in the game thought deliberate hands was a bookable offence in any part of the field. Soon the assessors were reminding the referees that a caution should only be administered when the offence denied the other side an advantage – as when a defender, realizing that he is the last man and a forward is racing past him, jumps to catch the ball.

Those managers who said that no players would be left to play the game by the end of the season because they would all be banned were talking codswallop, but they would not admit it.

The *Daily Mirror* started a League table of referees. The man at the top was the referee who had handed out the most bookings. I was halfway. That George Best sending off gave me extra points!

When one of the referees near the top, Brian Daniels, did a QPR v Fulham match and failed to caution anyone, a QPR supporter sent him a 'Get well' card. But it wasn't funny. The referees were only applying the laws and carrying out orders. The *Mirror* dropped its table.

Slowly the beneficial effects of the campaign began to be seen. George Best, now that he had been saved from suspension, could turn on the ball and take opponents on without fear of being hacked down. Geoff Hurst no longer had to spend half the week on the treatment table having his back seen to. Most significant of all, the attendances began to rise. The fans must have liked to see the ball players, such as Marsh, Best, Willie Morgan and Don Rogers, given their chance to show their skills. A player like Southampton captain Terry Paine suddenly found his career being extended. Alan Gilzean, supposedly on the way out at White Hart Lane, was still scoring goals at the age of thirty-four. It was nonsense to say that physical contact was taken out of the game. The hard tacklers could still tackle without being penalized so long as they connected with the ball first.

Steve Perryman, the Spurs midfield player, is one of the best tacklers in the game. The new, stricter application of the laws has not affected his style much. But the player who tackled 'through' an opponent and said 'I was going for the ball' soon accepted that he was on the stop list. You still had to be a man, not a fairy, to play professional football. But players who infringed now knew they had to accept the consequences.

The row rumbled on. The players were still very angry and wanted a meeting with the League and the FA to talk it all over. A meeting was called in London in mid-September and we all talked all day. The League knew they were right. But at this stage, the players were refusing to admit it.

The League's campaign was supported by the Minister of Sport, Eldon Griffiths. 'Over the last few years the reputation of the professional footballer has been given a black eye by the behaviour of some stick-at-nothing players,' he said. 'That has to be put right.'

Arrangements were tentatively made for another meeting with the parties because a rift still existed. That meeting did not take place for two years. The only side eager to continue talking was our side, the referees. Perhaps the players and managers did not like the truth. At the first meeting Bob Lord, chairman of Burnley and a member of the Football League Management Committee, told the managers that it was their fault. They could stop the professional foulers if they wanted to.

I agreed with Mr Lord that the managers had a great responsibility. The tactic of standing on a ball at a free kick, for example, which was being coached by some FA Coaches in schools, was a good example of how some managers and coaches were helping to make football less attractive to watch. The idea of awarding a free kick is to give the other side an advantage. If the kick is taken quickly, a goal often results. But if someone is allowed to stand over the ball, and all the defenders and forwards get back too, there is no advantage. The ball is cleared.

The professionals in the game answer, why should they give an advantage to the other side? The reply to that is, if both sides were allowed to take free kicks as they should be taken – quickly and without argument – both sides would gain the advantage. The extra goals would be shared out.

The player who was told to 'make it hurt' in his first tackle to deter a ball player of suspect temperament would now find himself in the book. Referees who never booked players in the first few minutes now cautioned them at any time – in the first minute as in the last.

A major criticism was that there was no uniformity among

referees. Some got their book out and others didn't. Well, is that surprising? If a film of an incident were shown to fifty referees it is obvious that not all of them would give the same verdict.

What looks a good penalty from one angle may not appear to be so clear-cut from the other side. Ask witnesses at a car-crash what happened and you invariably get different versions. What appears to be an innocuous foul to the TV cameras and spectators may seem much more serious to the on-the-spot referee, who can gauge the intent by the player's facial expression or what he says.

A good example of this use of discretion came in the Hull v West Ham FA Cup tie in 1973. Jimmy McGill, the Hull player, was coming away with the ball when Clyde Best, the West Ham forward, caught him from behind. McGill, a quick-tempered player, began abusing Best and both men squared up, though no blows were struck.

'What you want to try and hit me for, man?' asked Best.

'I'll give you hit me,' said McGill. 'Kicking me like that.'

I let them talk it out. I could understand their frustration. There was a lot of atmosphere and tension at Boothferry Park that day. Then I said, 'Right, now we've got that off our chests, let's get on with the game.'

There may have been a memorandum from the Football League on what to do and not to do, but referees still used their common-sense. Most referees prefer to talk quietly to a player and warn him. Next time, the player knows he could be in the book.

This is the reason why the crowd react so noisily when they see a player cautioned for what appears to be a not-too-dangerous offence. They are unaware that the referee has already given a warning.

The talks that took place among referees before the start of the clean-up succeeded in one respect – they achieved uniformity in many aspects of refereeing. For example, most referees now take up the same position at penalty kicks, corner kicks and other dead ball situations. This is a positive development for the good of the game. The co-operation between referees and linesmen is greater now than it has ever been.

Some referees disagreed with the clean-up campaign and

several, like Danny Lyden, resigned. They thought it was taking away their individuality and making them conform to the same pattern. Others objected but swallowed their pride and carried on.

It is impossible to get eighty-three men to think the same way. Some people will never conform. Eric Jennings, the ex-Cup Final referee, would never follow the party line. Even when the Football League banned long white sock-tops for referees because they might clash with those of the players, Jennings still persisted in wearing white.

It was also laid down that referees would not take out their books unless they were actually intending to caution a player. To take the book out as a threat and put it back was not to be done any more. Jennings stood out against that too.

Two years after the campaign was launched there were still people in football who refused to admit that it was a good idea. Under the new disciplinary points system introduced in season 1972–3, players knew that certain offences warranted a penalty of so many points. And twelve points meant a two-match ban. It was a less harsh system than the old one, which saw players banned for eight weeks or more. But the moans about referees continued. There was still too much gamesmanship, too many professional fouls and too much dissent from players. I always enjoyed refereeing. But I enjoyed it more after the clampdown. There was more skill being expressed by the players.

I think at the back of the players' minds was the thought that referees being stricter meant taking away one of the traditional rights of the English game – that it was a man's game and you could go in hard. The footballer looked on his right to tackle an opponent in much the same way as Americans, or most Americans, jealously guard their right under the Constitution to own a firearm.

But there was a fair way and a foul way to tackle opponents. The referee, the man in the middle, had the tough job of having to distinguish between the two. Referees are human, as are players who make mistakes. Referees slipped up on occasions. But the overall result of the clampdown was favourable. The game was better for it.

9

The George Best case

The five words George Best said to me at 8.12 on the night of 18 August 1971 caused me more torment than any incident in my refereeing career. My life was threatened by cranks. And after sending Best off for violent conduct, I had the impression that the soccer bosses were embarrassed by my actions. They would have preferred me not to have sent him off.

The decline in attendances was beginning to accelerate. George Best was the biggest attraction in the game. Millions of children worshipped him. For him to be banned from the game for a long period would have been catastrophic. Well, that was how it was presented to me.

I looked forward to taking that Chelsea v Manchester United game. I always enjoyed a Manchester United match, home or away. The gates would often be closed before the start. The atmosphere was made.

It was no different on 18 August. I arrived at Fulham Broadway underground station at 4.30, three hours before the kick-off. I never go by car to a London midweek match because of possible traffic delays. Even at 4.30 the queue stretched half-a-mile up Fulham Road.

I went straight to the referees' room, which was next to the away team's dressing-room. Sometimes you could hear what the players were saying in their dressing-room. Since then, however, the old stand has been demolished at Stamford Bridge and a new one has been built. No doubt with a sound-proof dressing-room!

Three hours was a long time to wait but it didn't seem long to me. This match had that extra spark about it. I was excited with the prospect. There were 54,763 fans inside the ground. Many of them were there to see Best, the current idol. I admired Best as much as any of them. He was a great player. I liked to see his ball skills. His balance was fantastic.

I was sitting having a cup of tea and reading the evening newspapers when the Conservative Minister of Sport, Eldon Griffiths, came in with Denis Follows, secretary of the FA. Mr Griffiths was a Manchester United supporter. The Football League's advice to referees to be stricter had just been issued. Mr Griffiths said he agreed with this. I had the impression that he thought this campaign should have started long before. 'I am in favour of being firm,' he said.

Half-an-hour before the start the two team-managers brought in the team sheets. Dave Sexton, the Chelsea manager, was friendly and chatty as always. Frank O'Farrell, of Manchester United, never said much. He was a quiet fellow.

Just before the kick-off I visited both dressing-rooms to give the pre-match talk. One of the things I said was that any player using abusive language to the referee or linesmen would be sent off. I said that deliberately and slowly so that everyone would understand. Once a referee allows a player to insult him to his face within the hearing of other players he has lost their respect. I would never tolerate this and I think most players knew it, because I had never had to send a player off for this offence.

I finished my talk by saying, 'Have a good game and enjoy yourselves.' I never asked for any questions as some referees did. You could make trouble for yourself that way. I believed in making a short, sharp speech, lasting only about a minute, and getting out. Footballers never liked the referee coming in, anyway. Referees were an encumbrance.

I felt in a good mental state for the game. There was a tremendous volume of noise from the crowd. The first half flowed smoothly. A United 'goal' was disallowed for offside when the linesman flagged. No one was angry about that.

The trouble began in the forty-first minute. Peter Osgood headed a cross to Tommy Baldwin, who scored. Osgood was standing behind a United defender and was close to him when he headed the ball. The United players claimed that their man had been pushed. I did not think so. I was in a good position to see. The players and the linesmen were in front of me.

As soon as the ball crossed the goal line I turned and ran towards the centre of the pitch. The linesman also ran back to the halfway line. This was standard practice which I agreed with all my linesmen before the kick-off. If you stand around in the penalty area you attract trouble. Some players will appeal about anything, but if there is no referee to appeal to, they can't do much about it.

Willie Morgan, Manchester United's Scottish international winger, came over to speak to me at the halfway line. He complained that there had been a foul and I had missed it. I took no notice. Denis Law tried to pull him away and so did Bobby Charlton. But Morgan persisted.

'If you keep on about the thing I will have to caution you,' I said. I gave him every chance. I did not take out my book straight away. Morgan kept on talking. I took out my book. 'What's your name?' I said. 'And the initial?' Morgan looked disgusted. He turned and walked back towards the centre. I was standing on the main stand side of the ground, the left side as Manchester United attacked towards the Shed. George Best came up, looking very agitated.

My recollection is that Best was looking right at me when he said, 'You are a fucking disgrace'; Morgan was some distance away, walking in the opposite direction. There was no doubt in my mind that Best was talking to me. Morgan did not react. If the words had been spoken to him, the natural thing for him would be to say something back.

I said to Best, 'What did you say?'

He replied, 'I wasn't talking to you.'

'Yes you were,' I said. 'What's your name?'

'Best,' he said.

'Initial?'

'George Best.'

I ordered him off. He was so astonished that he sat down on the pitch holding his head. He didn't say anything. Some of the other players came to commiserate. They looked contemptuously at me. I wasn't happy about it either. Thousands of people there had come to see George Best. Now, after forty-two minutes, he was to play no further part in the game. But I knew I had done the right thing. Law 12 is quite clear about violent conduct and using that sort of talk to the referee comes under 'violent conduct'. The punishment is sending off. I could make no exception. The laws were the same for George Best as for the least known Fourth Division player.

Players had expressed disgust many times at my decisions in other matches. I accepted that because I believe that in a pressurized world like that of professional football people sometimes explode. But to come up to an official and say what Best said, as I thought, to me, went far beyond that. No referee likes to send a player off. It is the ultimate decision. You cannot call him back.

The reaction from the crowd was awful. They booed non-stop. They probably thought I had ruined their night's entertainment. As we went off at half-time the Manchester United players avoided me. Police came out to escort us in.

The referees' room was a miserable place. We weren't gloating over the sending off of such a great player as George Best. Hardly a word was said. I imagined that the United dressing-room next door was an equally dismal place. Whatever happened in the game now was unimportant. The talk afterwards would all be about why Best was dismissed.

There was a change in the players' mood in the second half. No one spoke. The game continued in silence. The crowd were much quieter too.

United improved. Chelsea didn't play so well. The result was 3-2 to United, a bad game for Chelsea to lose, especially as United had only ten men in the second half.

I was glad to blow the final whistle. Usually I go towards the tunnel and wait for the linesmen, so that the police can escort us off. The players have to pass us and most of them shake hands and say things like 'thanks ref'.

But this night none of the players even looked at me. The United players still looked angry. It was as though I was Judge Jeffreys. The Chelsea players did not acknowledge us either. They had been beaten.

When we arrived back in the dressing-room I threw the ball down. 'What a bloody disaster that is,' I said. There was a knock at the door. It was Frank O'Farrell. The Football League

91

forbid managers and players to go to the referees' room after a match.

'You know, Mr O'Farrell, you're not supposed to be in here,' I said. 'Please don't cause any trouble.'

'All I want to know is, what happened?' he said. I took out my card and showed him what I had written down. I asked him to leave.

He was a nice man and I did not want to see him involved in any trouble, so I said, 'Just don't say anything about your visiting my room and I won't report it.' He then left.

I was under the shower a few minutes later when Denis Follows knocked and entered. He did not speak about the Best incident but I told him about it. 'Anyone who talks like that has got to go off,' I said. Mr Follows accepted that.

In Chelsea's dressing-room along the corridor Dave Sexton was so upset about Peter Osgood's performance that he put him on the transfer list. That was the second sensational development of the night.

I was not worried about my safety when it was time to leave. There were lots of reporters standing outside but I didn't think there was anything I could say except that it was all in my report to the Football League.

Outside the main doorway some fans shouted abuse but none of them seemed as though they wanted to hit me! There were fans still standing about in the streets and at the underground station. They seemed stunned and most of them failed to recognize me. I was relieved. I didn't want to get into any arguments.

Next day the telephone never stopped ringing. Some of the language used was absolutely revolting and filthy. Several callers said: 'We're going to get you, just wait.' My wife, who took some of the calls, was appalled. I thought to myself: what does it mean? What have I done wrong? It was as though I had been guilty of a serious offence myself, like child beating. I was being hounded for doing what I thought was my duty as a referee. All this for £10.50!

Eventually we had to take the telephone off the hook. Down at the shop everyone who came in wanted to talk about George Best. One little boy who had been coming in religiously at the same time every morning to buy a packet of ten cigarettes for his father used to buy some sweets with the change.

But this time he said guardedly, 'Ain't you the feller who sent George Best off?' I said, 'Yes, that's right.'

'Well, I ain't coming in here any more', he said. Since that day that little boy has never been into my shop. I could imagine millions of children feeling the same way all over the country. I must have been the most hated person in soccer at that time.

Several photographers and reporters arrived and wanted to take my picture and interview me. I told them there was nothing to be said. I had sent my report to the authorities – two copies to the FA and one to the Football League.

I was selling jigsaws of George Best at the time, and one of the newspapers offered me £50 to pose next to one of them. I refused. Some of the correspondents in London were blaming me for the affair. Others were forecasting a long ban on George Best because he was already under a suspended sentence.

Scores of letters started to arrive, most of them so disgusting that I had to destroy them. I asked the village postman to parcel up the ones addressed to 'Burtenshaw, Football League referee, Yarmouth' and hand them to me separately so that my wife and children wouldn't see them.

There were many articulate letters as well. One person from Malden in Essex wrote:

Were you informed by the FA, as I am convinced many referees are, to 'get' the incomparable G. Best? It is not he that brings the game into disrepute but the omnipotent referee and the archaic way the FA run things.

I think it is disgusting that I will be deprived of watching this greatest of players for twelve weeks. I get tremendous privilege watching this unique performer displaying his skills for Manchester United. And I am certainly not going to watch football during his suspension. I pay money travelling all over the country to watch him, not to see referees continually on his back for trivial things whilst he gets continually kicked and battered about.

If he wasn't so fantastic he would have had a broken leg by now. I have seen Best sent off twice but never have I

93

seen a player sent off for despicably trying to kick Best off
the field. Justice? I think not.

What has he done to incur this iniquitous treatment –
wealth (good luck to him), long hair (jealous), being immeasurably? better than anyone else in this country (dis-
appointing)? What referees do not realize is that, believe it
or not, Best is human like any referee, like any member of
the Disciplinary Committee. Everyone makes mistakes, even
referees, but poor Best must not make a mistake else
authority comes down upon him like a ton of bricks.

When G. Best has gone from the game millions of people
will recall with excitement his playing days. Will anyone
recall the referees who have helped banish him from the
game?

I was grateful for that reference to Best being human like
any referee. I was beginning to doubt whether referees were
human! A former Army officer from Godalming made a request for me to be lenient:

In the cold light of day you probably now realize that you
awarded an excessively severe punishment for a harmless
incident. Please, before it is too late, can you not in your
report to the FA play down this incident to its correct
proportions?

As one of those present in the stand last night, I would
also like to remind you that the moment Best advanced to
speak with you the crowd, most of whom were Chelsea supporters, started cheering and coaxing him on to open his
mouth a little wider than perhaps he should have done.

I am no personal friend of Best, nor have I spoken to
him in my life. I am merely one of the many people who
pay for a seat and enjoy watching highly skilled professional players in action. I like to see a fair do for all but last
night's incident has the makings of something far beyond
the realms of justice, unless you yourself can institute some
remedial action.

Of course there was nothing I could do. I was there to administer the laws of the game. It was now up to the FA to
take whatever action they thought fit. No plea of mine could

make any difference. I couldn't go to the hearing and say, 'Sorry, I made a mistake.'

It was interesting to note that the Army officer saw Best come over and talk to me and not one of his fellow players. That would be a crucial point at the hearing. Perhaps the FA should have called this man as a witness!

There was just one letter of support from a Manchester United fan from Wilmslow. 'I am sure that the true lovers of the game support you, even if they make least noise,' he wrote.

The noise from the other lot was still deafening. The phone continued to ring. The piles of letters kept being handed over at the doorstep. Life was still a misery.

My next game was at Crystal Palace. Before the kick-off I met the then chairman, Arthur Wait. He said the FA couldn't suspend Best. It would be bad for the game generally. Clubs would lose 10,000 off their gates. I replied that no player, however great he was, could be immune from the laws. There could not be a separate set of laws for different classes of players. I felt that Wait's view was being supported by more and more people inside football.

The following week I went to a Rothman's 'Golden Boots' lunch in London. One of the players selected in the Great Britain side to receive his golden boot was George Best. But there was to be no confrontation. George Best didn't turn up. But his manager, Frank O'Farrell, was there. He shook hands. 'Is it worthwhile being so involved?' he asked, referring to the Best incident. I replied I still felt the same way. I had a duty to perform. If a referee ever felt like ducking out of doing his duty, he had no right to be on the Football League list.

The FA Disciplinary Commission that dealt with the Best case met at the Great Western Hotel, next to Paddington Station, on the afternoon of 13 September 1971. There must have been nearly a hundred Pressmen and TV men present. Some American tourists were eager to know what it was all about. One lady came up to me and demanded: 'What is your name, sir? Are you a film star or something?'

When I told her I was a Football League referee she was no longer interested. At first the Press didn't recognize me but when they did I had to dodge into the toilet. When I came out I saw the members of the Commission coming out of the dining-room. It crossed my mind that they must have had a good lunch. I had had nothing except a cup of coffee. I had left home at eight-thirty in the morning. My expenses for meals would come to £2.50 and my payment for giving up a day's work would be £10.50, the same as the match fee. Those referees who have their own businesses or highly-paid jobs, lose money when they come to these Disciplinary hearings.

By now the two linesmen had arrived. We were all called into Room 13, which was being used as the waiting-room. There were three chairs placed at one end and four at the other. The linesmen and myself occupied the three chairs. The other four were supposedly for George Best and his witnesses. What a farce! Everyone in the same room.

There was a clatter outside, the door burst open and struggling through a mass of bodies came Best, Cliff Lloyd, the secretary of the Professional Footballers' Association, Frank O'Farrell and Willie Morgan. We all looked embarrassed. No one spoke. They sat on the four chairs and we sat on our three. We tried to avoid looking at one another.

A man from the FA stood holding the inside of the door. Did they think we were trying to escape, I wondered. After ten minutes Mr Lloyd and myself were asked to go into Room 8, where the four-man Commission was sitting. When the door opened, the photographers fell in and we had to fight our way through.

Inside Room 8, I sat at one end of the table and Mr Lloyd sat at the side. The Chairman, Mr Vernon Stokes, asked Lloyd if he was representing George Best. Mr Lloyd replied that he was.

Mr Lloyd objected to the composition of the Commission. He said he thought it should be made up of men who were unaware of Best's previous record, otherwise the present case might be prejudged.

Mr Stokes replied that it was impossible to get such a Commission. Everyone knew George Best's record.

Mr Lloyd then started his case. He referred to my pre-match talk. Was it true that I said anyone using abusive language to the referee and linesmen would be sent off? I said it was true.

Lloyd: 'That means that the players could use abusive language to each other?'

I said it had not been my intention to tell them that they *could* use abusive language. All I was telling them was what they could *not* do, namely, use abusive language to me or the linesmen.

The members of the Commission had my report in front of them. It said:

> I have to report that I sent off G. Best of Manchester United FC for violent conduct. The incident which came under my notice was as follows:
>
> A goal had been scored against Manchester United and I had moved from the penalty area to a position a few yards inside the field of play on the centre line. G. Best came towards me and said 'you are a fucking disgrace'.
>
> My first pre-match instruction in the dressing-room was 'any player who uses abusive language to the linesmen or myself will be sent off'.

There was also a copy of a statement from George Best. This read:

> I have read the referee's report and can only say he has completely misunderstood the position. What happened was:
>
> A goal was scored and I returned to the halfway line to my position at outside-left to line-up for the kick-off. The referee was speaking to W. Morgan and then as I stood on the line he passed me followed by Morgan to whom I remarked 'fucking disgrace'.
>
> Immediately the referee turned round and said, 'What did you say?' I replied: 'I wasn't speaking to you'. Whereupon he said 'Yes you were, what's your name?' He took my name and ordered me off the field.
>
> My remark was not intended for the referee. Mr Burtenshaw had his back to me when I spoke to Morgan, having walked past me towards the centre of the field. I would like a personal hearing.

Mr Lloyd asked for the football field and Subbuteo men. This is a green cloth representing a football pitch, which is spread

97

out on the table with models of players. It was standard practice to use this children's game at Disciplinary hearings where witnesses had to place the central characters in their right positions. I put the Subbuteo men in the positions where we were standing at the time of the Best incident.

Mr Lloyd said, 'Are you sure about that?' I replied that I was.

Lloyd: 'So you weren't facing Mr Best at the time.'

Burtenshaw: 'Yes I was.'

Lloyd: 'But you have placed that player facing the other way.'

Burtenshaw: 'I wasn't aware that Subbuteo men had faces.'

I was surprised by this. But the point had been made. An elementary slip like that might now prejudice the whole case even though both linesmen would give evidence in support of my claim that Best was facing me.

The first linesman was called, Mr M. J. Thorpe. His report stated:

I have to report that the referee sent off G. Best of Manchester United FC for foul and abusive language. The incident which came under my notice was as follows:

The above player in showing dissent to the referee's decision used foul and abusive language to him. This occurred approximately in the 42nd minute of the match. The referee then sent the above player off the field of play.

Both teams had been informed by the referee in their dressing-rooms prior to the match that any player using foul and abusive language to a match official would be sent off the field of play.

Mr Lloyd asked the linesmen how he had heard Best use foul language when he was quite a way from the incident. The linesman replied that he had been told this.

Lloyd: 'In other words, it was hearsay.'

Mr Stokes intervened that it was common practice for the referee and linesmen to consult about incidents, but in fairness he felt the linesman's evidence should be ignored.

The second linesman, Mr D. A. J. Ling, was called. His report was slightly different. It said: 'Best appeared to exchange words with the referee.'

Mr Ling was asked to place the Subutteo men. Like me, he wasn't sure which way the faces went, and had himself facing the stand. Mr Shipman helped him.

The next witness was Willie Morgan. He said he had been cautioned for dissent, and as George Best passed him, Best made his 'f... disgrace' remark to him. He confirmed that Best was facing the opposite way to me.

The chairman asked me if I wanted to ask any questions. What was the point? I was only a witness. I wasn't the prosecuting counsel.

Frank O'Farrell was the next witness. He positioned the players in a similar way to Morgan. Mr Lloyd asked him what happened after the game. Mr O'Farrell said he went to the referee's room. I was amazed that he wanted this to come out. We had agreed not to mention it because O'Farrell could have found himself in trouble with the Football League for going into a referee's room after a controversial incident.

There were no further questions. I didn't feel it was up to me to try and cross-examine O'Farrell on the points which disagreed with my own evidence. No one cross-examined him, so that was how it was left – a very unsatisfactory state of affairs and not the way that justice, any kind of justice, whether soccer or in the civil courts, should work.

Mr Stokes asked if Best had anything to say. Mr Lloyd said he hadn't. Mr Stokes said, 'Surely he wants to say something?'

Best then positioned the Subbuteo men and muttered a few words. No one asked him any questions. There were things I could have asked but the Football League policy was to advise referees not to do so.

Mr Stokes asked us all to wait in Room 13. We filed out and when we got back in the waiting-room resumed our seats. Us at one end, them at the other. I went up to the man guarding the door and said couldn't we have a cup of tea. He said yes and went to order it.

When the tea arrived, we pulled our chairs up to the table. 'Surely we can have a cup of tea together?' I said. We sat there for forty minutes making half-hearted attempts to talk. Best didn't say anything.

We were called back but only for more evidence about the positioning of the players. Back to Room 13.

O'Farrell, Lloyd, Morgan and Best huddled close together, talking in low voices. Once again the call came. We went into Room 8.

This statement was read out:

Having heard all the evidence the Commission is not satisfied beyond reasonable doubt that George Best directed the words complained of to the referee. They were foul and contrary to rule 12, and would call for stricter punishment in view of the referee's pre-match talk when he warned players that he would send off anyone who used abusive language to him.

In his evidence Mr Norman Burtenshaw conceded this could have led players to think they could use it to other players.

The Commission was satisfied that the sending off of George Best was sufficient punishment and the existing suspended sentence would not be implemented.

Best was ordered to pay the cost of the Commission. I was flabbergasted. What kind of justice was that? I knew Best had spoken to me and not Morgan. I could not understand it. What did I send him off for – to make myself a hero and create an impression? To get myself in all this bother? To have my life threatened and my family's lives made a misery?

Best didn't say anything but he looked pleased. As we turned to leave, Mr Stokes called me back. I was reluctant to go back. I didn't want any homilies from him.

Mr Stokes is a nice, well-intentioned man but I was angry and he could see it. He said he thought I was not particularly helpful during the hearing. But the explanation why I was reluctant to add to my report was that Mr Hardaker, secretary of the Football League, always advised referees: 'Don't go beyond your report at the hearing.' This was advice that I always followed at FA hearings.

I walked out without another word. I was seething. A few days before the Best incident the League had launched their campaign to clean the game up. One of its primary purposes was to protect players like George Best from tackles from behind and unfair treatment. Now when a case came before the Commission, the referee wasn't supported. Back in the waiting room, I told the linesmen, 'He got off.' We claimed our expenses and left.

Best was quoted later as saying that he was now finished with trouble on the field. 'I am determined to do everything I can to avoid this sort of thing again. I would be lying if I said this business hasn't worried me. It has. I am so relieved that it is all over. I am sure it will be easier for me now to keep control. This referees' clampdown is a great help.'

Next morning I rang Denis Follows to tell him what I thought about the handling of the case and the parts of it which disturbed me as a referee. It seemed that everything possible had been done to get George Best off. No effort was made to try and substantiate my action. The whole purpose of the hearing was designed to prove me wrong.

Follows said, 'You had better come down here to see me.' Next day I paid my own expenses to go to London.

I said, 'The Commission completely chickened out of their responsibilities.'

He was sympathetic and said, 'If you had asked me I would have come as a witness to the commission, I was at the game, as you know.'

I wondered about that. He could have given evidence that Best was facing me. So could that fan who wrote to me. So could thousands of people if only they had been called. But there were no witnesses for the prosecution, only me and the two linesmen, one of whom had been scrubbed out because he had been too far away to hear what was said.

I also spoke to Mr Hardaker and George Readle before my meeting with Follows. Mr Hardaker said: 'I realize how you feel. Why don't you take a deck-chair down to the beach and have a sit down and relax?' I got the impression they weren't too pleased with the outcome of the case.

I don't think the other Football League referees were happy about the Best case. No referee could be happy about it.

I think a lot of people had a conscience about that case. Later, at a joint meeting of the referees, the Football League and the PFA, I met Mr Shipman and Mr Stokes again. Mr Stokes complimented me on my refereeing of the 1971 Cup Final and added that he felt I still had something to learn about conducting myself at personal hearings.

101

There was an ironic sequel to the Best case. On Saturday, 3 February 1973, I met Frank O'Farrell again at the Hull v West Ham FA Cup fourth round tie. He had just joined West Ham as a scout after being sacked as manager of Manchester United.

He talked about how it felt to be out of work. How he had started doing the washing-up at home again. And then he said something which surprised me.

'I felt very sorry for you over that Best business,' he said. 'I can understand just how you felt.'

There was no more to be said.

10

Danny Blanchflower, what did I do to upset him?

The Sunday after the George Best case Danny Blanchflower wrote a big piece about it in the *Sunday Express*. Everyone had got it wrong. It wasn't George Best's fault at all. The guilty men were Alan Hardaker and myself.

Blanchflower started off:

> I am in no mood to mince words. Rarely have I been so angry about injustice on the football field. On the Tube to Chelsea v Manchester United I read reports of a revolt by club managers against referees and the manner in which they were carrying out recent Football League instructions to clamp down on dissident players.
>
> 'They can't have it both ways', Alan Hardaker, the Football League secretary, was quoted as saying in response to the protests. 'If they want the game cleaned up and controlled firmly then this is just what they are getting'.
>
> Trust Hardaker. As Football League secretary he has licence to make some of the all-time idiotic statements on the game. No, Hardaker, nobody wants it both ways. We want it one way, the fair way, the proper way.

Blanchflower then wrote about his excitement at going to an early-season game when the grass is green and the colours of the players' shirts look cleaner. Then:

My hopes dropped when Norman Burtenshaw ran out with the whistle. He is not my favourite referee. There is no personal reason. I hardly know him. But on the field he irritates my instincts for the game.

The irritation is common to other players. He angered Arsenal last season with a goal decision at Elland Road. The Benfica players attacked him at Highbury. He has caused more trouble than most players but never been suspended.

At Stamford Bridge he disallowed an early goal for Manchester United. It looked good to me. But the linesman raised his flag quickly and Burtenshaw ruled out the goal. I wondered why he did not consult the linesman, but I gave him the benefit of the doubt.

There was no doubt about Chelsea's first goal. Osgood clearly fouled a United defender – pushing him in the back – before Baldwin scored from Osgood's header. Burtenshaw seemed to be in a good position to see it. If he did, and he should have done, he ignored it. It was a clear injustice to United and some of their players reacted to it. Morgan, the nearest, made a mild-looking protest. Burtenshaw booked him.

I wondered how Blanchflower could tell that it was a mild protest. How could he hear, sitting in the stand a long way off? But to continue:

Charlton and Law made appealing gestures to the ref for common-sense. He stood rigid and stone-faced. George Best, taking up position for the kick-off, looked more incensed and determined to rile Burtenshaw. What he might have said to the referee is conjecture but his attitude was just as stupid as Burtenshaw's.

He confused the issue. He made himself the scapegoat of Burtenshaw's folly. He gave too many people the distraction of partially defending Burtenshaw's justice when there was little in it to defend.

Blanchflower then went on to moralize about the increase in violence in the world and in soccer.

The teams have been getting more brutal and determined,

more professional if you must call it that, and the referees have had no opportunity to keep step with this march of time. Not having had the same professional chances to improve as the players, and having no deep instinct for the development concerned, they have not been able to maintain the balance and keep the growth of it within reasonable bounds. Consequently they have become a much maligned and criticized group. But the fault lies with the administrators and their inability to see the shortcomings.

I reproduce Blanchflower's comments at some length because they show another of the pressures on the big-match referee – the influence of unfair criticism in the Press. After reading that, can many readers of the *Sunday Express* doubt that I must be something of an idiot? Can players have had much respect for me after reading it?

I was so annoyed that I spent £80 on getting the advice of a Queen's Counsel to find out if the article was defamatory. I was advised that it would be costly to press ahead with a case, so I dropped it. I spoke to Alan Hardaker and he too was rather upset by some of the comments.

'Give him enough rope and he'll hang himself one day,' he said. Blanchflower's criticism was no worse than many attacks on me in the newspapers but I resented it more than the others because it came from someone who ought to know better, a former player who knew how players behaved, a former player who should know the laws of the game.

I wondered whether his attack might have been a legacy of the only incident I can remember concerning Blanchflower on the field. It occurred when I was refereeing a Spurs match against Birmingham City. Blanchflower criticized one of my decisions. I told him: 'I don't tell you how to play, don't tell me how to referee.'

It was the sort of exchange that takes place regularly on the football field. You think nothing more about it. But at the end of the game Blanchflower came to my dressing-room to apologize. I told him there was nothing to apologize for; I had forgotten all about it.

One newspaper had a headline following the Spurs v

Birmingham game: 'N for Norman, no N for Nelson because he missed so much.'

In my view referees get far too much unwarranted criticism. If the referee adds on time for time-wasting, as Mike Kerkhof did in the West Ham v WBA game in 1973, and a goal is scored in the extra time, the referee is the person who gets the blame, not the time wasters. If there is any kind of controversy about a goal, it is usually the players' side which is presented in the newspapers.

Managers will sound off about referees. 'That man has undone a season's work,' Leeds manager Don Revie said about Ray Tinkler. Only one section of workers in the football industry attracts more harsh criticism than referees – managers of struggling sides.

I cringe when I read some of the things written about them. Often the position of their team is not their fault. It may be due to the players; or the directors. How often do you find directors being attacked in the newspapers?

Relationships with the Press are vital to everyone in the game because the Press is the link with the paying public. In my view, contacts between the Press and referees are totally inadequate. Both sides are at fault.

On the referees' side there is a reluctance to talk to newspaper reporters because so often a remark has been distorted or taken out of context and made to mean something else. My FIFA colleague Pat Partridge talked to a reporter once about a Liverpool v Manchester City FA Cup tie and was horrified to see the headline 'Top Ref Slams Allison'. In fact, Partridge hadn't mentioned Allison. I have been quoted myself when I haven't even spoken to the reporter concerned.

Most referees make a point of telling their wives to say they are not at home on Sundays, because that is the day when the national daily reporters ring. Unless you know the reporter and can trust him to discuss incidents off the record if necessary, you are unwise to say anything.

The Football League don't ban referees from talking to the Press. But they frown on it. And if something appears in print which they don't like, the referee could be in trouble.

On the Press side, I think there is a feeling that more contact with referees could benefit everyone, and I certainly agree with this. Often I come out of a ground after a game in which there has been a mysterious-looking caution and I am amazed that no one tries to find out what it was all about.

There seems a hesitancy on the part of the reporters, as though they feel they are doing something wrong. I think the Football League should get the clubs themselves to overcome this lack of information by appointing a liaison officer to come into the referee's room after matches and be briefed about incidents.

This liaison man could take down an official statement about why a referee cautioned a player and what he wanted to say about it. There would be no trouble then about misquoting. Everyone would have the same statement.

At the moment, all that happens is that the referee hands a list of the players cautioned or sent off to a club official who is supposed to have it read out to the Press. Personally, I would be willing to conduct informal Press conferences after matches provided that reporters would quote me accurately and observe any restrictions about parts of the conversation being confidential and unattributable. I recognize that with a dozen or more reporters involved, this may be impossible to achieve.

There are a number of football writers, like Blanchflower, who were players themselves – Trevor Bailey of the *Financial Times*, Tony Pawson of *The Observer*, both outstanding amateur players, Ivor Broadis of the *Newcastle Sun* and Bernard Joy of the London *Evening Standard*.

Joy is very respected and I gave him many quotes in my time. But being helpful to him on occasions didn't save me from getting some stick following the Jackie Charlton goal at Leeds. 'He brings his book out like a pompous schoolmaster,' wrote Joy. Was that really necessary? How does the referee bring his book out?

I do not think that it is a good thing to have so many players writing about the game. If a player has retired from football and trained as a journalist, like Joy, then okay, but I believe the professional in each field should be given his chance. No professional journalist should be squeezed out because his newspaper has hired a sportsman who can't write but talks to someone who can. No journalist ever gets selected for a First

Division club on the strength of his written work, so why should a footballer be picked for a writing job?

Among the Sunday papers, *The Sunday People* is the one most of the referees buy because it gives them marks out of ten like the players. How a journalist can sit down and assess twenty-two players and a referee and give them marks at the same time is beyond me!

I remember a reporter coming into my room once and asking for some information about a caution. 'Which paper are you from,' I asked. '*The People*,' he said.

'I never get less than nine in *The People*, you know,' I said. Next day, there it was at the end of the match report – nine out of ten!

Some reporters, like Maurice Smith, tend to mark high. I always did well when Maurice was at a match. Others, like Mike Langley, marked low. Langley gave me four on the strength of one controversial incident once, but I must say he did give me ten for the FA Cup Final.

Are all reporters qualified to judge referees anyway? Of course they aren't! Do they know enough about positioning and picking up, off-the-ball incidents? About the comments referees make privately to players? And the other technical aspects of refereeing such as co-operation with linesmen and the use of advantage which only qualified referees would know about?

Referees always joke about their *People* marks, but there are a lot of people who take them seriously. Friends have said to me: 'I see you had a bad game last week.' When I asked if they were present they replied: 'No, but you only got six in *The People*.'

There is a handful of journalists qualified to judge because they are referees themselves, for instance, Max Marquis of *The Observer*, Leslie Vernon of *World Soccer* and *Rothman's Book of Football* and John Parsons of the *Daily Mail*.

As with football itself, the standard of football journalism has improved immeasurably in the last few years. The newer reporters understand more about the game, but I feel few of them understand much about the problems of referees. Some, like Ken Jones of the *Sunday Mirror*, don't seem to want to. Jones gives me the impression of being anti-referee.

There is a saying among referees that if they have survived the Monday morning papers they have had a good game. The Sundays have discussed the match fully and often, if there is a controversy about a goal, all the Mondays have left to have a go at is the referee.

The *Daily Express* has a system of marking matches from one to five which sometimes baffled me as much as the *People* marks. Sometimes I would do a match which I thought was splendid entertainment only to find the *Express* man had given it three. The *Daily Mail* also has an Entertainment League which judges matches purely on entertainment value.

The newspaper which I prefer to read is the *Daily Telegraph*, because it gives more space to discuss the match as a balanced whole rather than deal with it in terms of controversial incidents. Donald Saunders is sound and David Miller, though much stronger in his opinions, is a good read.

Sometimes referees find themselves on the receiving end of fulsome praise. This happened to me after the Chelsea v Stoke League Cup Final. J. L. Manning of the *Evening Standard* even rang me up to congratulate me. He wrote a piece which was most complimentary to the two linesmen and myself.

Frank Nicklin, sports editor of the *Sun*, once wrote a 'Burtenshaw was great' article in his newspaper, but my opinion of Mr Nicklin changed abruptly a year or two later after having an uncouth conversation with him on the telephone!

Do the Press do justice to the game? I think football gets a vast amount of publicity which sustains mass support for the game, but I also feel that there is too much criticism of individuals, not just referees and managers but players too. This criticism reflects the worst prejudices of the fans who, being on the outside, don't appreciate the problems and pressures of the modern game.

Some reporters understand these problems and it is reflected in their writing, but there are others who sit apart from the game and pour too much abuse on it. These people destroy, or try to destroy, Sir Alf Ramsey. They write continually about the good old days of football as though the present game is worthless.

There is much to decry in modern football but it is mainly

the things that the Press miss – like cheating, time-wasting, feigning injury, bad sportsmanship, verbal abuse on the field and the so-called professionalism of teams intent on winning irrespective of the harm they do the game. The standard of play and general fitness is better than it has ever been. There is a levelling out of standards. Perhaps fewer great players but many more good teams.

Often the criticism hits the wrong targets. In my last season, for example, Matt Gillies, the manager of Nottingham Forest, was given some terrible stick before he finally got the sack.

It was the kind of criticism which hounds good people out of the game. Billy Wright experienced it at Highbury. So did another Arsenal manager, George Swindin.

Wilf McGuinness was never allowed to get going at Old Trafford; and when Frank O'Farrell got the sack, how many critics attacked Mr Louis Edwards and his fellow directors?

Fans are entitled to criticize because they pay for the privilege, but I sometimes think journalists could show a greater sense of responsibility. In my last season, Don Howe, so successful as a coach at Arsenal, was experiencing this type of written abuse at West Bromwich Albion.

In 1973 Dick Graham resigned as manager of Colchester and went out of football, another example of a good man being lost to the game. I remember a story about him when he was manager of Crystal Palace. As I came out of my dressing-room, Cliff Holton, then captain of Palace, was just about to lead his team out. 'Come on lads,' he said. 'We've listened to what the manager has had to say. Now let's go out there and do the opposite!' Everyone had a good laugh.

11

'Franny Lee Had a Hand in It'

I made 124 decisions in the Tottenham Hotspur v Manchester City match at White Hart Lane on Saturday, 10 February 1973. One of them, in the seventy-fifth minute, made me the laughing stock of the nation on TV, to quote the Spurs captain Martin Peters.

Tony Book, the Manchester City right-back, crossed from the right and Francis Lee scrambled the ball over the line at the near post. I thought it was a good goal and pointed to the centre. Immediately four Spurs players ran at me shouting that it was hand ball. I was in yet another row.

Spurs v Manchester City would not have been my first choice match if I had had the pick. I knew most of the Spurs players because I toured Japan with them. I liked them and got on well with them. But I had some difficult moments in the past with the Manchester City players and their manager, Malcolm Allison.

I was more tense about the match than I was normally. There shouldn't have been too much tension. Neither side was in the race for the title. The previous Wednesday night, Spurs had led Derby 3–1 in the FA Cup tie at White Hart Lane but lost 5–3 in extra time. So they would be feeling low.

Manchester beat top-of-the-table Liverpool 2–0 the same night in another FA Cup tie. So they would be feeling pretty good. They put out the same side. Spurs had two changes –

111

Joe Kinnear for Ray Evans at right-back and Jimmy Pearce for Ralph Coates on the left.

I caught the 9.40 train from Norwich and had breakfast on the train. I changed trains at Liverpool Street and boarded a local train which stops at a station called White Hart Lane, only about three hundred yards from the ground. It was 12.40 when I arrived at the ground. I didn't have lunch. I never do before a match. I sat about talking to the club secretary and other people who were about.

Then I went to the Spurs dressing-room for some laces and saw Eddie Baily, the Spurs assistant manager. Bill Nicholson, the manager, was at the Manchester United v Wolves match. It was unusual for him to be away. Baily was in charge in his absence. I always liked Eddie Baily. He is one of the game's leading characters.

'Have you seen the other lot's studs?' he said.

I said I hadn't. 'They're as long as this,' he said, holding his thumb and finger wide apart.

I told my linesman to have a look at the Manchester City studs. When he came back he said, 'Yes, they're very long. I don't think I've seen such long studs.'

'Are they legal?' I asked. The stud gauge which all referees had been given to measure studs and make sure they were the specified shape and length had been withdrawn by the Football League because at that time most of the boot manufacturers couldn't comply with it. It was up to the linesman to make a decision on his own initiative about what was legal and what was not.

'Just about', said the linesman.

I could hardly go into the City dressing-room and tell the players they couldn't wear them. 'If they're not dangerous, that's all right,' I said.

The pitch was soft but not really heavy. A crowd of 30,944 was inside the ground; not big by Tottenham standards and there were huge gaps on the terraces.

At 2.20 Allison walked in with the City team sheet. The regulations laid down by the Football League stated that both managers should come in together with their teams at 2.30.

'I'm sorry, I can't accept that,' I told him. 'You know the rules.'

He didn't say anything. He walked out. He was the only manager who used to come in on his own. Why did he persist when he knew it was against the regulations? Allison was never a conformist!

A few minutes later he came back with Eddie Baily and handed the sheet over. It had the names of the eleven players, the substitute and the colours on it. Once the sheet is handed over, you're not supposed to change the side.

The bell went for the teams to get ready. City went out first in their blue strip with Continental-style flashes. Spurs went out a minute later. There was little reaction when I ran out with my linesmen. There rarely is.

I went straight to the centre and blew my whistle. Colin Bell, the City captain, came up with Martin Peters, the Spurs captain. They wished each other a good game, and I threw my 1966 polished penny up and Bell called correctly. I have used the same coin since England won the World Cup. The teams changed ends.

It was slightly blustery. City kicked with the wind. It would be difficult with long kicks from the goalkeeper. Judging whether a player is offside from these kicks is one of the hardest tasks the officials have.

It was a quiet opening. In the second minute Mike England, the Spurs centre-half, pushed Bell and I blew for a free kick. Two minutes later England headed out for a corner.

I didn't have to blow. All the players accepted that it was a corner. But there was a dispute in the fifth minute when City goalkeeper Joe Corrigan dived on the ball on the dead ball line. The linesman looked unsure. I couldn't tell from my position inside the penalty area, so I waved play on. Some of the Spurs players were indignant. But you only give what you see. Neither the linesman nor I was certain it went out.

Mike Doyle, the City midfield player, went down injured and I stopped the game. It started to rain. The surface of the pitch became skiddy. That doesn't help in judging tackles. Steve Perryman slid into Rodney Marsh and I gave a foul.

Mike Summerbee, the City winger, had the ball taken off him. Doyle was the nearest player. 'What about the fucking man on then,' shouted Summerbee. If someone had warned him that a tackle was coming, Summerbee would have taken

113

evasive action. There was a surprising amount of bickering between players of the same side.

Offside against Spurs. Cries of 'Watch the game, ref.' The game was pretty dull with really bad passes. The crowd made little noise.

Marsh appealed for obstruction by England. Marsh gives the appearance of saying a lot on the field but it is all mime really. He doesn't make a great fuss, unlike some of the City players. It was a half-hearted appeal.

Martin Peters was booed for pulling out of a fifty-fifty ball with Tony Towers. The first goal. Eighteen minutes gone, and it brings the match to life. Tony Book, the thirty-eight-year-old City right-back, nips in to intercept a pass from Jimmy Pearce. The Spurs defence is coming out and is caught as Book's low centre sweeps across the area.

Francis Lee lets it go on Marsh's call, and Marsh shoots as the goalkeeper, Pat Jennings, goes down at his feet. The ball rebounds, hits Marsh in the face and goes into the net with Cyril Knowles trying to kick it out. I point to the centre and set off upfield.

The linesman flags for a push by Tommy Booth, the City centre-half, on Chivers. Spurs have the ball so I let them have the advantage. More cries of 'Watch the game, ref.'

A foul against Doyle for pushing. He pats me on the back. 'Watch it,' I tell him. 'Okay ref,' he replies.

Joe Kinnear, the Spurs right-back, tackles Lee from behind and Lee is upset about it. I give the foul and tell them to get on with the game.

In the twenty-fourth minute Corrigan kicks downfield and Marsh chases after it ahead of the Spurs defenders. The linesman has flagged for offside, so I blow. The City players sound off. I was thirty yards away. But the linesman was right there. Marsh indicates that he started inside his own half and couldn't be offside.

It's a tough one for the linesman. He has to watch the goalkeeper for the moment the ball is last kicked and at the same time watch where Marsh is. The strong wind doesn't help.

A second or two later we have a repeat of the same incident. This time the linesman doesn't flag and Lee goes on with the ball. The crowd shout for offside. Lee shoots and Jennings, off his line, puts a big hand on the ball. Lee falls over him. He doesn't claim a penalty.

Book tackles Pearce and I give a foul. The crowd chant: 'You're a bastard referee.' You get that at most grounds. Marsh, running alone, suddenly falls over. Perhaps it is those long studs!

The thirty-second minute, and Spurs start to come to life. Perryman hits a long ball from the right towards goal and Booth lets it go, expecting Corrigan to come out. But Corrigan is slow, and Martin Chivers jabs out his foot and the ball goes into the net to make it 1-1.

Chivers is away again. A run on the left and a pass inside to Pearce, who turns and shoots against the near post. The ball bounces into Corrigan's arms. Just as he catches it, Cyril Knowles charges into him. Angry reaction from the City defenders. I blow for the free kick and Corrigan, a huge man, six feet four and fifteen stone, collapses on the ground.

'It was a fifty-fifty ball!' cried Knowles. I gave him to understand that I didn't think it was as bad as it looked.

'You were a bit late,' I said. 'Watch it in future.'

He continued arguing. 'Just cool it,' I said. The City players didn't seem too excited, so they must have thought the same way as I did.

Whenever Spurs had a goal kick, Chivers would push up, forcing the Manchester defenders back. He knows the laws. He can't be offside from a goal kick. Chivers never says a lot on the field. He is one of the best-behaved players. He takes stick but never loses his head.

The last two minutes of the half were quiet. I added on three-quarters of a minute for injuries. At half-time the linesmen and I talked about the offside problem from the long kick outs. It would be easier if the wind dropped.

The second half was delayed to 3.57. One of my new laces broke and I had to change it! In the forty-seventh minute, Beal forced his way past Tony Towers and Towers fell over. Some people might think it was a foul. I didn't think so. It doesn't make any difference to me whether it is a home player or an away player. I know referees are supposed to be biased in favour of the home side because of the influence of the crowd. I try not to be.

Beal went on and passed to Alan Gilzean, who was in a good position on the right. Gilzean beat one defender. Now he was ahead of the last defender. His skill had put him into a wonderful position to score a goal.

But before he could shoot, Willie Donachie, the City left-back, hacked him down from behind. It was the worst kind of so-called professional foul. I got my book out straight away. Donachie didn't say a word. He knew it was inevitable. The free kick from Peters was headed against the far post by Chivers. The next time Donachie touched the ball he was booed; and the time after that.

Rodney Marsh down again. Appeals for foul against Beal. I wave play on. In the fiftieth minute City have a corner, and while Summerbee is preparing to take it I notice John Pratt having a go at one of the City players. I don't stop the play. But when the ball goes behind for a goal kick and the players push up, I speak to Pratt.

'I saw that. Just watch it.' It is the best way to handle it. If you stop the game and lecture him the crowd react aggressively because they might not have seen the incident. They will be saying 'What's the twit held it up for now?' If you let it go, it could lead to retaliation off the ball later. Fists could be flying. I want the other player involved to know I saw it too.

Lee falls on Kinnear after pushing him, and the crowd think I am warning Lee as I walk over to them on the touchline. But I don't say a word. All I'm doing is seeing that they get up gently and don't do anything stupid. That's the advantage of being up with play. If you are a long way away from an incident like that, the players can start grabbing and mauling each other.

The fifty-second minute and City score their second goal. 2-1 to City. Marsh goes up the left, sends Kinnear the wrong way at the near post and pulls the ball back towards Lee. Pratt, trying to pass back to Jennings, sends it into Lee's path, and as three defenders close in on the ball, Lee forces it home. No arguments about that!

Knowles and Marsh go up for a high ball. Marsh goes down. I give the free kick. Knowles is enraged. 'I never touched him. He never jumped. You must be able to tell when a player doesn't jump.' I say nothing. The game goes on.

Thirty-two minutes to go and City start time-wasting. Corrigan takes a long time to decide where he is going to kick the ball. I point to my watch from the centre circle to tell him I am adding time on.

There is a bit of a pantomime over a goal kick. Three City players walk past the ball leaving it where it is so that Corrigan has to go and get it. More time-wasting!

Doyle takes a throw and the ball doesn't go into play. The linesman flags and I can't understand what he is flagging about. He shows me. He gives the throw again.

Perryman tackles Marsh. The crowd roar. They think Marsh is conning. I give the kick. Chivers passes to Pearce on the near post and Pearce, realizing that the way ahead is blocked, backheels the ball to where I am running in. He must think I am a player.

'Sorry,' I say. Two players are pushing each other at a corner.

'Is it necessary to stand on exactly the same square foot of grass?' I ask them.

Booth goes down injured after a challenge from Gilzean. It might be quite bad, because he is lying still. The Manchester City trainer comes on. Nothing much seems to happen. I use the time to ask the linesman on that side to change his orange fluorescent flag with the linesman on the other side, because it is clashing with a man's orange coat on the terraces.

I wondered why I wasn't picking up his signals too well. I run over to the other linesman with the flag. When I get back, Booth is still down.

I say to the trainer, 'Can we make an attempt to start the game?'

'Don't shout at me,' he replies.

'Can we get him off,' I say civilly.

'I haven't had time to decide what the injury is.'

'Well, you've had some time. All I'm trying to do is get the game moving.'

Eventually Booth gets up and the game restarts. Kinnear is injured in a tackle with Lee. Coates, the substitute, starts warming up.

The seventy-fifth minute. Book breaks free on the right and I am not far behind him. He centres low to the near post and

Lee dives in. The ball goes into the net. I was in a good position to see.

I point to the centre. The linesman is already running back to the halfway line. That is standard procedure. If the linesman thought there was something wrong with the goal he would have flagged.

Immediately I am beseiged by Spurs players. Peters grabs me by the arm and won't let go. He is screaming: 'Hand ball. He handled it.' He pushes me into Mike England, who is standing behind him. Knowles and Beal are also there.

They are all shouting. 'See the linesman', they shout. I say to Peters, 'I haven't come out here to be pulled around by you or anyone else.' I reach for my book. Peters is not far off being cautioned for abusive language and ordered off.

The sight of the book coming out begins to quieten them down. Peters lets go of my arm.

'What's your name?'

'Peters.'

'Initial?'

'M.'

The conversation continues. Five policemen are behind the dead-ball line, patrolling the terraces there. The crowd chant: 'Go home, referee.'

Peters says: 'You'll be the laughing-stock of the nation when they show it on TV.'

The BBC are filming the match for *Match of the Day*. I don't care what the TV film shows. I don't have any playbacks. I give a decision because I think it is right.

Apparently Marsh is telling the other Spurs players that Lee admits handling the ball. And Lee says to one of them: 'I'm in the running for the Sportsman-of-the-Year award so I'll own up to it.'

But I do not learn this until after the game. In any case, I don't rely on what people say. I call it the way I see it. And I can see nothing wrong with the goal.

One Spurs player impresses me with his demeanour – Jennings. He doesn't say a word. He accepts the decision. It must be just as frustrating to him as it is to Peters if he feels that it wasn't a goal, but he is taking it like a sportsman. I wish there were more players like him.

Spurs want to bring their substitute on. I go over to the other side of the field as Pratt goes off and I check that the linesman has seen Ralph Coates's studs. If it was a hand ball, the crowd don't seem to be reacting in other parts of the ground.

The game starts again. Gilzean won't stop talking about the goal. He keeps on chipping away.

'Why don't you give it a rest,' I tell him. The seventy-ninth minute and Peters heads a cross from the right back and Chivers whacks in into the net, 3–2 to Manchester City.

As he goes back to the centre Peters runs up. 'I hope for your sake that other goal isn't the winner,' he says. I don't know what he means by that.

The crowd are excited now, spurring their team on. A high ball leaves Peters on his own. He shoots against Corrigan's legs but I have already blown for offside. Peters says nothing.

Another offside against Spurs, and Chivers is angry. Not with me but because of the way the City players are wasting time. I tell him I am adding time on.

Offside against Lee just over the halfway line. He picks the ball up and slowly walks towards Mike England. Then he drops it as he holds it out. The crowd shout their disapproval. They know when players are deliberately wasting time. I warn Lee again.

I add on three minutes in the second half – two minutes for injuries and one minute for time-wasting. There is hardly any noise from the crowd. They are turning to make their way out of the exits. There are none of the usual boos for the referee.

I stand by the side of the pitch waiting for both linesmen. Three or four policeman are hovering nearby. No one comes on to the pitch. It is quiet.

The players are talking among themselves. Peters comes up to complain again about the Lee goal.

'I've got a living to make, you know,' he says.

That makes me angry. 'Yes, and I am getting £10.50 for making an honest decision,' I reply.

What kind of living is he making? A much better one than I am. His basic is probably ten times as high as mine. Anyway, what has his making a living got to do with me giving a goal? Am I depriving him of his living? I am disappointed with his attitude. He is the captain. He should be giving an example to the other players.

We go into the dressing-room. A man comes in who says he is the liaison officer between the club and the Press. I had never heard of that before. He wants to know which players have been cautioned. The Press thought all four Spurs players in the row might have been booked. I tell him only Peters and Donachie; Peters for dissent and Donachie for that tackle from behind.

An hour after the finish I come out. There are a dozen or so reporters waiting in the car park and as many friends of the players. No one tries to speak to me. There is nothing much I can say, anyway.

As I walk up the High Road towards the station, fans are standing around on the pavements. They recognize me but no one says anything. If they thought it had been hands you would think they could muster a boo or two. I have washed my hair. With this wind, I might get a cold!

That night I went to a meeting of the Referees and Linesmen Association's excutive at the Windsor Hotel in Lancaster Gate, just one hundred yards from the FA headquarters. The others asked me how I got on.

'Had a controversial goal. That's nothing,' said one. 'I gave two penalties, one against the home side.' We had a laugh and a chuckle. You wouldn't think we had been involved in such tension earlier in the day. I felt exhausted. Not with the running I had to do in the match – though it was probably more than usual – but because of the mental strain.

It hadn't been a bad match, except for the one incident. There were 27 fouls, 12 goal kicks, 53 throw-ins, 9 corners, 12 offsides, two stoppages and five goals. The only unusual statistic was the goals. Five was a lot for a First Division match. The previous Wednesday there had been eight in the FA Cup replay at White Hart Lane. So that was thirteen in two matches.

Over a drink before dinner, the referees chatted about their matches. One said he was waiting for a free kick to be taken when he turned and saw a player in the wall suddenly fall to the ground with blood pouring from a bad cut on his mouth. Someone had hit him on the quiet. Of course no one knew who it was. The player had to go off for stitches.

Sheffield United v Birmingham City – a different view of the relegation
battle as referee Norman Burtenshaw dives in to break up a fight between
United's Mick Speight (No 11) and City's Bob Hatton. Hatton was
sent off.

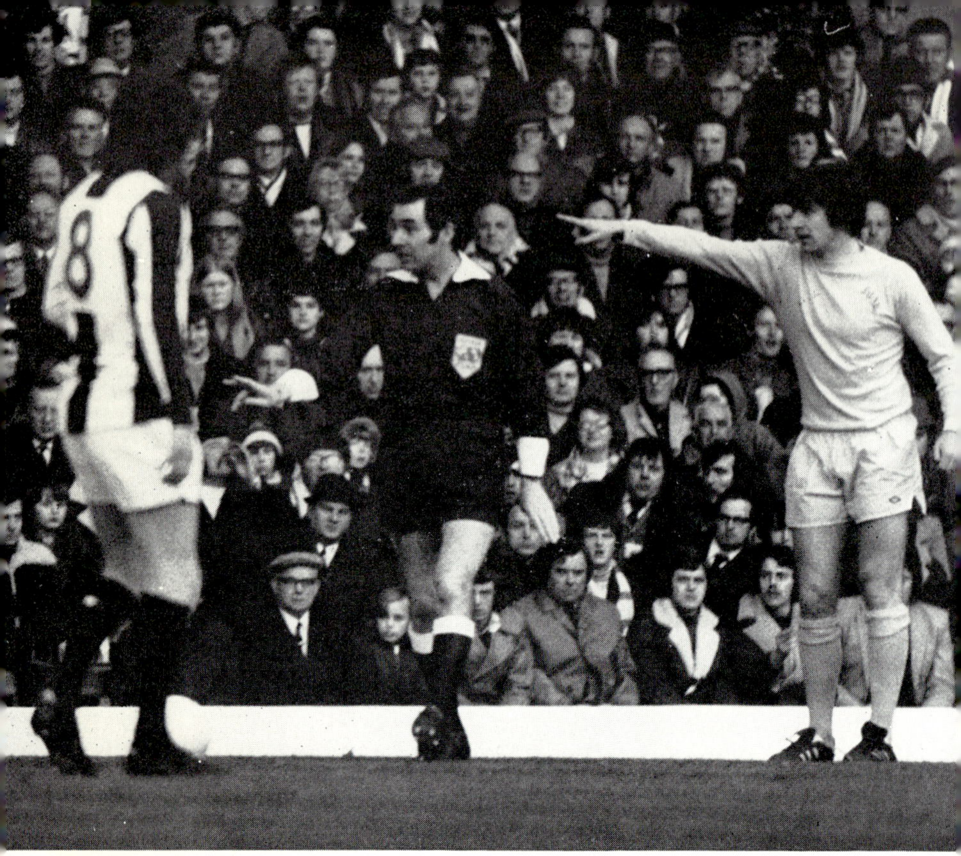

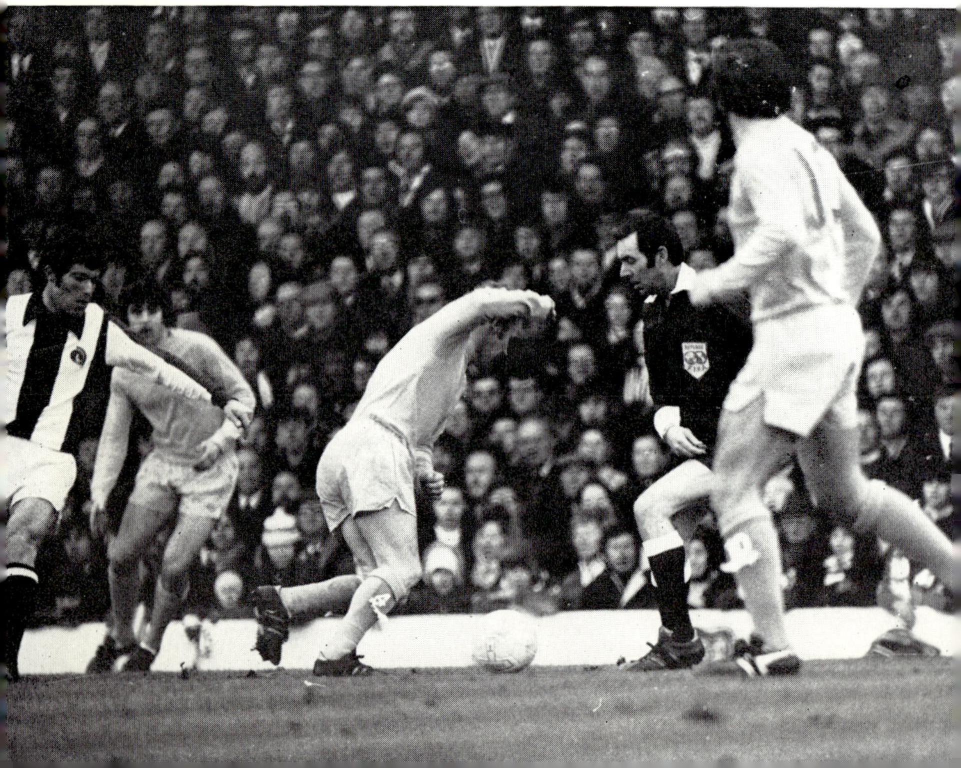

Above: George Best holds his head. He can't believe that he has been sent off. Tony Dunne (left) and Bobby Charlton escort him. It's the second day of the so-called Refs' Revolution in August 1971. The match: Chelsea v Manchester United at Stamford Bridge.

Above left: Peter Lorimer (Leeds) complains about the tackling of WBA's Alistair Robertson in an FA Cup tie at Elland Road in 1973. Burtenshaw warns Robertson: 'Cut it out'.

Below left: Occasionally the referee can be too close to the play. Leeds captain Billy Bremner has to do a ballet act to avoid Norman Burtenshaw.

Above: Even great goalkeepers break the laws sometimes. Referee Burtenshaw warns Gordon Banks about his conduct.

Below: Peter Osgood (Chelsea) lectured for treading on Stoke City centre-half Denis Smith in the 1971 League Cup Final. Osgood was cautioned.

My friend Keith Styles of Barnsley – a very witty character –
told a good story. He had done the Watford v Blackburn game.
A player was tackled outside the area and went down. The
ball ran loose and one of his colleagues banged it into the net,
but he didn't know.

'What about the foul, ref?' he said. 'Diabolical! Aren't you
going to give it?'

Said Keith: 'You want me to disallow the goal?'

Player: 'Have we scored? Ignore everything I ever said!'

After dinner we started our meeting and it went on for
three hours, so we missed *Match of the Day*. Not that many
referees ever see it; they don't get back home early enough.

It was after midnight when I went to bed. Next morning I
was up at eight to attend another meeting at nine. It had been
a hectic weekend. I wondered whether Martin Peters was doing
any voluntary work like this.

It's not that I am jealous of Martin Peters earning £100 or
more a week basic, or whatever it is he earns at Tottenham
Hotspur. But like most referees, I am angry when we are
attacked and our motives and honesty questioned. We are
doing a professional's job for a pauper's wage. The wage,
£10.50, makes us appear amateurs.

Every man at that meeting was a top man with nearly
twenty years of experience as a referee. We had made no
money out of it. We did it because we loved the game and
being involved in it.

The Sunday newspapers had versions from the City players
about that goal. 'Frannie had a hand in it, you can say,' Marsh
was quoted.

He may have done. I don't know. All I know is that I didn't
see it. I couldn't give something I didn't see.

Peters complained in Monday's *Daily Express* that all he
was asking me to do was to speak to the linesman. Instead of
doing that, he said, I went to the other linesman to check
Coates's studs. Perhaps if footballers knew that the linesman
is told to stay upfield and signal if he sees an infringement,
Peters wouldn't have said that. There was no signal from my
linesman and he turned to go back upfield when the goal went
in, as I tried to do.

Francis Lee had a column in Tuesday's *Daily Mirror* in which he said:

No, I'm not suffering pangs of conscience about my grand act of larceny against Spurs at White Hart Lane on Saturday.

And before you howl 'cheat' let me explain why I didn't confess to the referee that I'd scored a false winner for City – with my hand.

If I had come clean, I would have been letting down my team-mates and my club. In the grim business of professional football, goals are jewels and if you have a chance of pinching an illegal one you are bound to do it.

A cynical attitude? Not if, like me, you're convinced that many attackers pot a dozen or more legitimate goals a season that are wrongly disallowed. Not when a single point splits the top four clubs in the First Division championship, as happened last season.

I feel sorry for the referee, Norman Burtenshaw. My after-match confession exposed him to ridicule, though he had done his job to the best of his ability.

But I can say, categorically, if he'd asked me on the pitch about the validity of the goal I would have owned up.

He didn't. He was thirty yards away at the time and I didn't feel justified in running over to him and arguing about his decision. That's the best way of finishing up in a referee's book!

So why embarrass Mr Burtenshaw after the match by admitting hand-ball? The simple explanation is, I was asked a question. And answered truthfully.

These things have happened before and if it happens to me again I will have the cheek to react in precisely the same way.

At least the man's honest! In the next day's *Mirror* Frank Taylor reported having attended a forum of the Bexley referees with Fulham manager Alec Stock. One referee asked if the modern player was a cheat. Mr Stock was very indignant. 'The game is cleaner today than it has ever been', he said. I wish I had been there!

Later that week, the Assessor's Report arrived at my house.

I reproduce it in full because it shows what kind of strictures referees suffer from. I have seen a wife of a referee burst into tears when she read one of these reports about her husband. It was so damning you wondered why the poor fellow ever became a referee. This is what my report said:

1 Application of laws and control. Your authority and control were well established during the first half but both teams by their tactics fully tested these during the second half, and you dealt with most situations in a firm and acceptable manner, except as mentioned in paragraph 4. Could you not have dealt more adequately with the Tottenham protests over the third goal? Having awarded what was a doubtful goal to the visitors, the home captain Peters remonstrated with you. You withdrew to the goal-line area (near the home supporters) instead of, as I thought you might have done, run upfield nearer to the centre.

2 Positioning and fitness. Whereas you revealed your usual high standard of fitness and abandoned the rigid diagonal to cover a great part of the ground, you nevertheless placed yourself in positions close to play but with your back to your linesmen.

My notes revealed you missed five signals (three from one linesmen and two from the other), as on no occasion were the signals acknowledged. With the abandonment of the diagonal, try and acquire positioning that will still keep your linesmen in a quick and clear viewpoint.

3 Advantage. During the opening half the advantage clause was applied with discretion, but after the interval the tone of the game had changed sufficiently to warrant the almost complete abandoning of its application.

4 Stoppages and signals. Your signals and decision-making were unmistakably firm and clear. You were not, however, equally firm with the Manchester City players during the final fifteen minutes when they blatantly indulged in time-wasting tactics.

5 Co-operation with linesmen. As already mentioned in paragraph 2, you were ill-positioned at times to observe your linesmen. Early in the game linesman Sheppard signalled that the ball had gone out of play for a corner kick. He was

ideally positioned on the corner flag to judge, but you chose to play on although you were facing the goal-line squarely and were some distance in the field.

When the third goal of Manchester City was scored, followed by the protest of home players, you were on the blind side of the scorer but once again linesmen Sheppard was well positioned on the corner flag.

But you chose not to consult him although I felt had you done so it might have appeased the home players, even though the linesman may have supported your decision.

All in all, the team work generally was not of the usual high standard, although both linesmen were complying with the agreed Sheffield Conference (1972) decisions.

6 General remarks and summing up. You were below your usual high standard in this game and not working well with your linesmen as in previous games witnessed. You also lacked firmness with the visiting players' time-wasting tactics of a varied but nevertheless obvious nature. Could you not have taken a more positive action than just indicating time was being added and the occasional 'hurry up' signal? There were provocative tactics as far as opposing players and spectators were concerned.

The game was certainly a hard one with difficult players in both teams. Your capabilities and efficiency are both qualified but not totally evident on today's performance. The exchanging of the linesmen's flags during the second half was a commendable and common-sense action.

Personally I never resented assessors' reports. I think they fulfil a purpose in helping younger referees and bringing older referees up to scratch if their marks are beginning to deteriorate.

However, I am not in favour of the top referees being assessed regularly unless they have done something to deserve being looked at and criticized. The assessor's criticism about not going to consult my linesman after the Lee goal was not really fair because I had already looked at him and he was returning to the centre circle – the usual agreed practice when the linesman thinks it is a goal. If the referee goes over to consult the linesmen, the players have a further opportunity to mill about protesting and shouting, which is undignified for the game.

As for the remarks about abandoning the diagonal, I did that because I wanted to be closer to possible infringements. Most of the linesmens' signals were missed because of the colour clash with the spectator's jacket, not because I wasn't looking.

And as for abandoning the advantage, as the assessor inferred I should have done in the second half, it it fine saying that from the stand but try telling it to the players. If you penalize every foul instead of letting the innocent player have the advantage, you have a start-stop game and the frustration builds up for players and fans.

Advantage is one of the trickiest things, anyway, for the referee to decide. When the ball is played up to the centre-forward and he lays it back – a common practice these days – the centre-forward will often appeal for a foul if he is pushed in the back by the centre-half as he plays the ball. But if the ball is laid back to another attacking player I usually give the advantage.

'There's something on for your side', I will tell the centre-forward.

I agreed with the assessor's views about time-wasting. I thought there was a lot of it during the second half. In fact, I told one player; 'We will be here until midnight at this rate'.

But what do you do? Do you start cautioning every offender? That would be farcical. The spectators wouldn't know what it was all about in most cases.

I think the Football League themselves should act over time-wasting. They should ask referees to report on the number of examples they come across in their matches. Clubs with a high number of incidents reported should then be fined. For these are the clubs who are keeping spectators away from football grounds and making the game a bore.

The Spurs v Manchester City assessor's report was a good example of report writing even though I disagreed with some of its comments. There were some complimentary ones from other matches!

The final word on the Francis Lee affair came from Brian Clough on 'Sportsnight with Coleman' a few days later. Clough was interviewed by David Coleman. He said: 'Francis Lee put the referee I consider to be the best in the country in an absolutely impossible position by owning up. I sincerely hope that in his next game he scores a purler of a goal. And some clown of a referee comes along and disallows it.'

The *People* gave me four out of ten for my performance in that game!

12
The High Court at Lancaster Gate

In my time as a referee I spent many hours attending hearings of the Football Association Disciplinary Committee. Usually they took place at the FA headquarters, a terraced, green-painted building in Lancaster Gate, off the Bayswater Road. The front of the building gets very hot because the central heating doesn't seem to be adjusted properly. At the back of the building it is much cooler.

The Disciplinary Committee gets a lot of criticism, though not as much as referees. Someone said that if the men who sit in judgement on soccer cases were High Court judges, the Kray brothers would still be at large and John Christie would never have been hanged. It must be admitted that an awful lot of footballers get off.

Mr Vernon Stokes, a solicitor from Hayling Island, is the chairman of the Committee. He is a very nice man who leans backwards, sideways and frontways to be fair to everyone. Sitting with him are twenty-four members of the FA and Football League clubs, dignitaries like Len Shipman, President of the Football League, Bob Lord and Mike Gliksten, members of the League Management Committee, and Brian Mears, chairman of Chelsea.

Despite the way players sometimes get off when often they know they are guilty, most are scornful about the disciplinary system. For years they ran a campaign to change it. They said it was against all natural justice to ban a man from his work for several weeks and deprive him of his wages, which is what used to happen to some players with bad records. Players like Denis Law, Brian O'Neil, Billy Bremner, Peter Osgood, Alan Ball, Ian Ure and Derek Dougan were all banned and fined in their careers.

When a couple of Fourth Division players were banned for eight weeks apiece there was a huge outcry and MPs even started talking about the unfairness of soccer justice. The men at the FA were really given some stick, although what most of the critics didn't realize was that if players behaved themselves according to the laws of the game they wouldn't have been fined and suspended. It was the players' fault really, not the men at the FA.

Football discipline even got talked about at Government level, when the Minister of Sport intervened. And when the referees' clean-up began in 1971, the men at the FA began to accept that change was inevitable. If the old system continued, hundreds of players would be out of the game and the clubs would have to engage bigger staffs.

That was when Mr Stokes and his colleagues came up with the idea of suspended sentences. Yes, the player was guilty and would normally go down for a month but because of the extenuating circumstances he would be fined £100 and given a suspended sentence of four weeks. If he got into no further trouble, the suspended sentence would lapse. But if he came back before the Committee, the suspended sentence would be added on to any further punishment.

That was the way it was supposed to work, but players with suspended sentences did come back and not all of them had to serve the extra time. Cliff Lloyd and his players on the PFA didn't like this idea much either.

So the men at the Football League sat down again and worked out another scheme and presented it to the FA. The Football League never liked the FA way of handling things. They wanted to do it their way. The man in the street couldn't understand the set-up anyway. Here were Football League players being disciplined by the Football Association, some of whose members were also Football League people; Len Shipman, for instance, belonged to both bodies.

The new scheme involved a points system – four points for a foul tackle from behind, four points for continued commenting to a referee concerning his decisions in an effort to intimidate him, down to one point for illegal marking of the pitch by goalkeepers (See Appendix 2).

Many of the penalties were aimed at stopping the professional foul. Shirt pulling was a three pointer. Wasting time was two. When a player recorded a total of twelve points – for, say, three deliberate trips in succession or six deliberate hand balls – he was automatically due for a two-match suspension. But he could ask for a personal hearing and appeal against any of his cautions.

Players could still be sent off for violent conduct, and the automatic suspension in their case was for three matches. They, too, could appeal.

No longer would players be fined for field offences. The old restriction on not being allowed to pay a player his wages during suspension was discarded. Few clubs ever kept to it, anyway. They always found a way round.

The players were supposed to pay their own expenses to hearings but usually the clubs paid. At one case I attended, a manager complained that the Committee's suggestion to hear the case again would cost the club money.

'Do you mean to say that the player is not paying his own expenses?' said the chairman of the Committee. There was an embarrassed silence.

To get round the PFA objection that there was no right of appeal for footballers – the prime argument of those Members of Parliament who fought against the old system – there would now be an Independent Appeals Tribunal.

This consisted of an independent chairman, Sir John Lang, a man from the FA and a man from the PFA. When the Independent Tribunal began work, players brought TV evidence and some still got off. Not that the referees minded all that much.

Our view was that once we had cautioned a player or sent him off, our work had been done. In effect, we were acting as the magistrate. The sentence was the administering of the caution. When a player appealed to the FA, that was like going to the Appeals Court in the High Court.

In the past, referees had been allowed to question the player at disciplinary hearings, but the Football League Referees and Linesmen Association told the FA that we hadn't brought the charge, so why should we fight the case? We were only there as witnesses. So the FA changed that and the members of the Commission themselves did all the questioning.

In those days the referee was allowed to claim for the amount of money he lost by giving up a day's work to travel to the Committee meeting in London, Sheffield, Manchester or wherever it was. It was not a very satisfactory system as many of us were self-employed. So the FA then introduced a new system of paying a flat rate of £10.50 for every hearing.

Football's disciplinary system appears unwieldly, and indeed it is unwieldly, as will be realized when I relate some of the things that happened to me. But it serves as a rough kind of justice which is far preferable to becoming like an ordinary civil or criminal court where so much time and money are wasted in legal arguments by solicitors, barristers and police. If I was a player, I would be reasonably happy with it. No football club would be content at having to pay out thousands of pounds in a season for legal expenses. It simply wouldn't be worth it.

The chief drawback of the system is that it is loaded in favour of the richer clubs who can afford to appeal and bring any number of witnesses and call for TV film. The Third and Fourth Division players cannot afford this on their £35 or £40 a week. And their matches are rarely, if at all, filmed by the TV cameras.

Another weakness is that the FA don't prosecute the case as hard as they should. They rarely bring witnesses to refute the evidence of the player's witnesses. There is usually an FA representative at every League match on a Saturday afternoon. Surely some of these men could give evidence.

There is also a Football League assessor at every League match, but only once to my knowledge was an assessor called as a FA witness. The FA rely on the evidence of the referee and the two linesmen, which is usually similar. A common objection from the players' side is that the officials have got together. Mr Stokes usually replies that this follows the pattern of police evidence. Inevitably there is a feeling that the officials'

130

evidence is slanted. Whereas if there were an independent witness, more notice could be taken of an opposing view to the one put forward by the player and his witnesses.

It is amazing how some players who have been fouled will come to Lancaster Gate and plead for the man who chopped them down and pretend it wasn't a very bad tackle. The inference is that the referee didn't know the difference between a bad tackle and a harmless one. Some players will plead that abusive language used to the referee was meant for a player instead and the referee got it all wrong!

An interesting case I attended in 1972 was Mel Blyth (Crystal Palace) v FA. Mel comes from Norwich and is one of my friends among the players. On Saturday, 4 November, I was refereeing the Palace v Everton First Division match at Selhurst Park in South London. I gave a free kick against Palace and the players moved back towards the edge of the Palace penalty area for it to be taken.

Alan Whittle, Everton's Under-23 international forward who a week or two later joined Palace for £100,000, said something to Blyth as they ran back. Blyth elbowed Whittle in the face and Whittle went down. I wasn't watching the ball. I was looking directly at the two players because I suspected that something like this would happen. I ordered Blyth off the field and he went without a word.

The Everton players protested that it should have been a penalty. I had to tell them that the ball was dead as we were waiting for the free kick to be taken, so how could it be a penalty. I admit I made a mistake when the game restarted. I thought the free kick had been taken. The ball was out of play by the touchline and I allowed a throw to take place.

After the game Bert Head, then Crystal Palace manager, was quoted as saying Blyth would not appeal. 'I would never condone that conduct,' he said. 'He committed an offence and was sent off, that is all there was to it.'

Blyth never argues with referees and had never been in any trouble before. He should have served a three-match ban, but over the weekend Crystal Palace must have changed their minds because Blyth asked the FA for a personal hearing.

I was quite sure he would fail. A blow was struck. The TV

131

cameras did not show the whole incident but many people at Selhurst Park that day saw what happened.

The Palace case was conducted by one of their directors, Mr Jim Swann. He must have had some legal experience because he cross-examined me on my evidence for forty minutes.

Mr Swann asked me which elbow Blyth had used. I said the right. He said 'No, it was the left'. This conflict of evidence seemed to sway the members of the Committee. I could not see why. A player had been struck. What did it matter which elbow struck him?

Chris Hassell, then the Palace secretary, was in the room as an observer. He is a very small man, roughly about the size of Whittle. Mr Swan referred to him so that the Committee could judge Whittle's size in relation to Blyth, who is a six-footer.

Mr Swann said that to a normal person, Blyth's elbow would hit the chest, not the face. Blyth said in his evidence that he was only attempting to shrug Whittle off. He wasn't intending to hit him. We all went out and when we returned for the verdict the chairman said the sending off was sufficient punishment. Blyth was acquitted. I was upset at the way the facts had been presented. But Blyth's clean record counted for a lot.

A short time later I did another Crystal Palace match. Blyth came in to see me before the match. 'That was a big con at the FA, wasn't it?' I said. He made no reply.

Another case which showed how the FA were keen to be as fair as possible to the defendant was the Denis Smith case in 1972–3. Denis Smith was the tall, fair-haired Stoke City centre-half whom I booked in a match at Stoke on 2 December for persistently infringing the laws.

It was a heavy pitch and Smith came in from behind and brought Chelsea's Bill Garner down. I told him he would have to watch himself. A few minutes later Smith brought Garner down from behind again, and I cautioned him for persistent infringement although the offence in question was not, in my opinion, worth a caution on its own, only in relation to the previous tackle.

At the first hearing the Committee said they were unhappy with the charge. Could two tackles be called 'persistent'? I thought it could but Mr Stokes doubted it. The Ernie Machin case had not been long settled – when the High Court upheld

Machin's appeal against a decision of the FA Disciplinary Committee – and Mr Stokes said he wanted to be fair to Smith. 'Perhaps we've got him here under the wrong charge', he said.

A member of the Committee cited the instance in a magistrate's court of a driver on a dangerous driving charge and the magistrates feel the evidence isn't strong enough to convict; and so the charge is watered down to 'driving without due care and attention'.

The Committee decided to try the case again under a reduced charge of ungentlemanly conduct. Smith was not guilty of persistent infringement but might be guilty of the lesser offence, which carried three disciplinary points as against four. Not that this made any difference, for even with three Smith would be up to twelve points and due for suspension.

Tony Waddington, the Stoke manager, was asked if he was willing to go ahead with the new case at that moment. He replied that he thought he ought to consult his directors first. So the case was postponed. When he left the FA building, Mr Waddington told reporters: 'I am rather confused. I am going back to Stoke where the air appears to be clearer.'

When the case was heard again a vital conflict in evidence came up which I thought might have clinched the case against Smith. The Stoke argument was that a long ball was played out of the Chelsea defence to Garner. I knew that it was a shortish pass because the linesman in that half of the field was close to the incident and gave evidence. If it had been a long ball the linesman would have been coming out with the Chelsea defenders. Like them he would have been many yards away.

This time there was a new chairman of the Committee, and Bill Garner, who had given evidence at the first hearing, was not present. The case took ten minutes. Mr Waddington asked me if I would have cautioned Smith for the second tackle if it had been considered in isolation from the first. I said no.

The Committee asked us to leave and when we came back said the action of the referee was right but the caution was not being recorded. In other words, Smith got off. The second 'trial' was an absolute waste of time.

An example of the crude behaviour that was creeping into football in the early seventies came in the Ipswich v Coventry match at Portman Road on 6 December, when I cautioned the

Ipswich captain, Mick Mills. Earlier that season Mills, who I knew to be a pleasant, friendly young man off the field, had made his debut for England.

In my report I wrote: 'A foul was given against Mills. The opposing player picked up the ball and lobbed it in the direction of Mills. Mills then made a "two-fingered up you" sign at his opponent. He then committed another indecent gesture which I was not alone in spotting'. The nearest linesman, M. D. Hutchison, was standing a few yards away near the halfway line and he reported:

'In the seventy-fifth minute I was running the left wing line with the Coventry forwards. Just inside the Coventry half of the pitch, towards the right wing used by the Ipswich forwards, M. Mills fouled a Coventry player and the referee penalized this foul. After the foul was given, the player Mills gave a V-sign and simulated the action of masturbating in the direction of the Coventry player he had fouled. His name was taken.'

This had never happened on a football field before, certainly not to my knowledge. I was amazed at a fellow like Mills reacting in this way. But I was in no doubt that Mills had made the gesture.

Mills, in his report, wrote:

A foul was awarded against me. The opposing player picked up the ball and threw it at me deliberately. His words to me at the time were 'here you are, you can have the ball.' I replied: 'I don't need it, we are 2–0 up.'

At the same time I indicated the score to the other player with finger sign language, i.e. two fingers indicating two and my other hand indicating zero.

No doubt Mr Burtenshaw, who was some distance from the scene, presumed I was making a two-fingered-up-you sign at my opponent and also indicating another indecent gesture.

I was really quite amazed when I had my name taken for the offence. I would be very interested to learn the interpretation of the linesman controlling that particular side of the field and who no doubt had a better and different view.

I estimated that I was four yards away from the incident. The linesman was not far away either. Both of us had no reservations. I took the book out because this was the kind of conduct that brought the game into disrepute. The incident had happened in front of the directors' box. Women were present. Was this the kind of conduct that professional football wanted to present to a mixed audience?

At the hearing the magnetic board – replacing the cloth of the George Best days – was brought out and we placed the players and officials where we thought they were standing at the time.

The Chairman asked Mills that if he was standing so close to the Coventry player why hadn't he used words to convey what he wanted to put across? Why use his hands to say the score was 2–0? Mills never answered that point satisfactorily.

Bobby Robson, the Ipswich manager, was very angry about the affair. He said it could leave a stain on Mills's good name. The Committee found the case proved and Mills was fined £50 and ordered to pay the costs.

One of the things that worried the members of the Disciplinary Committee was the way players appeared to use the appeal system to make sure they would be available for important matches. If a player who was playing in a vital Cup tie on the Saturday was due to begin a suspension on the previous Monday, he would appeal in order to play in the match. This 'professional' use of the appeals system annoyed the Committee.

There was a strange case early in April 1972 which didn't come into this category but was baffling all the same. I was due to appear at a personal hearing asked for by Allan Clarke, the Leeds forward. It was not long before the FA Cup semi-final against Birmingham. If Clarke had lost, he could have missed that match.

An official from the Football League rang me the day before the hearing and asked whether I could take the Fourth Divison match between Hartlepool and Southport. I said I had the Clarke hearing. The official told me to ring the FA and get it cancelled. I did that. I then realized that the Hartlepool v Southport match was the only game on that night. Why had I been selected? There were eighty-odd other referees available. It was a 352-mile trip. There may well have been a perfectly good and valid reason for asking me to do it; I don't know. But

Clarke played in the semi-final and later withdrew his appeal.

The case of Warwick Rimmer, the Bolton defender, showed how many defects there were in the FA system. Rimmer was sent off on 13 November 1971 for kicking an opponent in the match against Chesterfield. I was attending a personal hearing asked for by the England and Manchester City forward Francis Lee, who is one player who appeals more than most.

When I arrived I was told that Rimmer's case would also be heard. No one had told me of this. One of the linesmen whose evidence would be important was attending another Disciplinary Committee hearing in Birmingham.

I said I had no objection to the case being heard provided the Bolton party accepted the linesman's written evidence. I left the room and I was invited to watch a film show in another case, an appeal by Norman Hunter.

Leeds brought a projectionist with them who showed a series of still pictures of one of Hunter's tackles. It was a unique cinematic presentation! By the time that case had been settled and the Committee were available for the Rimmer case again, it was 5.10 pm and one of the three members of the presiding Committee had left.

Mr Stokes asked if it was a sending-off case. That should have been clear from the start, but still. The man from the Bolton Football Club presented a three-page statement. I had not been shown this statement before, nor had the members of the Committee. I could imagine the reaction of a defending solicitor in an ordinary court to that!

The statement was the longest in my experience of refereeing. In it, Mr Rimmer said he was born on 1 March 1941, was married and had three children aged four years, three years, and six months. He had played for Bolton for sixteen years.

His version of the incident was that the other player had rapped him on the ankles. 'This was deliberate on his part and most unnecessary and uncalled for. I immediately turned round and shouted at him. I cannot remember what I said exactly but I am absolutely sure that I did not swear. When I turned round, I admit I was very cross and very annoyed and I squared up as though to kick the opposing player who was still on the ground. However, I very sensibly stopped and did not kick him. Mr Burtenshaw the referee came up to me and said "an early bath for you. What is your name?" By way of protest I said to Mr Burtenshaw, "I never kicked the player." He did not listen to my protest.'

Jimmy Armfield, the Bolton manager, submitted a two-page statement in which he said he thought his player had been sent off for disagreeing with me. I had not seen this statement before. Nor had the members of the Committee.

Tea was brought in. The Bolton man said his club had written several letters to the FA about the case, which the FA had agreed to put before the Committee at the hearing. Mr Stokes hadn't heard about these letters. Nor had I. They were not read.

The Bolton directors put up a good case but I had the feeling that the FA had helped them by not sticking to their laid-down procedure.

When the Bolton man finished his submission, Mr Stokes intervened to tell him he had not said enough about Rimmer being provoked.

The Committee found the case proved but felt Rimmer had been provoked and the sending off was sufficient punishment.

I do not think that if footballers appealed to the High Court they would get better justice than they get at Lancaster Gate. The men who serve on the FA Disciplinary Committee are extremely fair and understanding men. But I do feel there should be someone from the FA presenting their own case the way a member of the PFA or the defending club presents the player's case.

I have a better idea – scrap the whole idea of cautions for anything less than the sending-off offences that apply now. Save all the trouble of getting the book out and going through the time-wasting, costly procedure of players appealing by giving the referee power to dismiss offenders from the field for a limited period, say ten minutes or even less.

This idea is not new. It comes from ice hockey, where offending players are sent to the sin bin to cool off. At the moment it would be contrary to the laws of the game to operate a sin bin in English football. But it is something that could be taken up and referred to the International Board. It could then be adopted worldwide.

No club would want to lose players for periods during a

match. As the present system stands, a player who is cautioned for one of the lesser offences stays on the field and his side is not penalized. This would eliminate the professional foul.

But if two players were 'sin binned' in the early stages of the match, the others would be pretty keen to behave themselves for the rest of the game. You can imagine the coach standing up and screaming for them to keep it clean!

An eminent QC who is a football fan, Louis Blom-Cooper, has supported this principle. He sees nothing wrong with it in law. The referee would have his authority restored. He would be the sole judge, which is the way it should be.

It would cut out gamesmanship and time-wasting and the other petty little ills that are creeping into the game. I am sure the referees would welcome it as an idea which would take a lot of the pressure off them. No referee likes having to give up time in the week to sit about at Disciplinary hearings waiting to give evidence.

Players who commit violent offences could still be sent off for the rest of the game and banned for a further match, subject to appeal to the Disciplinary Committtee. More and more players and officials are coming round to supporting the 'sin bin' idea. I think it is worth a trial.

The players themselves wanted the points disciplinary system which the Football League introduced. But they abused it by making cynical appeals in order to free players for vital matches.

Everyone knew what was happening; the same clubs kept appearing at appeals and the FA was being criticized for the breakdown, but surely the clubs themselves were guilty.

13

Did you see that on the box?

Referees are not supposed to like the televising of football because it can expose them and show up their mistakes. The argument about play-backs of controversial decisions has been raging for several years now and is likely to continue for a few more.

My view about TV football is that I like it and I think it is generally good for the game. Techniques of filming the play have improved so much that I am sure many supporters – especially those packed in on the crowded terraces at big First Division matches – see more of the match at home.

Colour TV has added a new dimension to watching football at home, and I feel this may be one of the contributory causes to the decline in attendances.

Televised football has helped raise the standard of play at every level of the game. Today it is possible for young park players to watch the skills of the world's best players, such as Pele, Beckenbauer, Netzer and Eusebio, at home on their screens. This was a privilege that was denied my generation.

Youngsters learn skills like passing with the outside of the foot from watching Bobby Moore do it. London Weekend Television employed an ex-player and former manager in Jimmy Hill to analyse the more skilful aspects of the game. Hill did such a good job that the BBC came after him. The BBC's commentators also do a good job but lacked the expertise of Hill.

I thought it was strange that whereas the BBC employed a

team of ex-cricketers to give opinions at Test matches – fellows like Richie Benaud, Jim Laker, Denis Compton, Ted Dexter and others – they never thought of doing the same at football matches. It was left to the commentator to identify, explain and comment all by himself.

Besides showing the good side of football, TV also showed its bad side. Like referees being jostled and having the ball thrown at them. Players arguing and fighting. The professional fouls. Deliberate time-wasting. And too many goals! So many goals were shown on *Match of the Day* that the average fan who went to see a 0–0 draw or a 1–0 game must have wondered whether it was worthwhile going to his match.

The BBC used to show a shot in their title captions of a referee cautioning a player and writing down his name. Surely that is not a side of the game they wanted to project?

I think the commentators are conscious of the responsibility they have to the game. For like the rest of us connected with it, they would all be out of work if there was no football.

ITV's Brian Moore is in my opinion the best. He qualified as a referee to improve his knowledge of the laws of the game and I think this comes over in his commentaries. He tries to explain why a referee made a decision instead of leaving the viewer baffled, as often happens on BBC.

I am amazed sometimes when I hear a commentator say: 'I don't know why the referee has done that.' The referee is not to blame. The commentator is. He should know what it was all about. Moore usually does.

The commentators suffer the same disadvantage as the referee. They cannot stop the action and work out where the move started and who handled the ball in the crowded penalty area. They have to make an instant decision.

Sometimes commentators read too much into a referee's actions. In one Leeds v Everton match Billy Bremner fouled Gordon West, the Everton goalkeeper at the time, and I blew for a foul. As Bremner ran back to the halfway line I ran with him, my usual tactic in this sort of situation.

'There's referee Norman Burtenshaw giving Bremner a wigging,' said TV commentator Kenneth Wolstenholme. In fact, I never said a word.

Wolstenholme was the commentator who gave me a bit of a

wigging earlier in my career. It was a match at Fulham. There was fog about. I had to make a decision whether to take a chance on the fog lifting and go ahead, or call the match off. I decided to postpone it.

Later, Wolstenholme was seen on TV saying that here he was under a sunny sky at Craven Cottage and referee Norman Burtenshaw had called the match off and everyone was very upset about it. By four o'clock, however, the fog closed in from the River Thames. My decision turned out to be correct. But you can never be sure. You lay yourself open to that kind of criticism.

David Coleman has since taken over as the BBC's top man. I never met him but I always thought he did a professional job in a professional way. I met one of the newer commentators, Barry Davies, frequently. He was about the only one who used to come into my room before the match to have a chat. I thought he was a very pleasant young man and I used to enjoy talking to him.

The Football League Management Committee discussed the effect of TV on attendances in the 1972–3 season and there was a general feeling that there was too much television. I thought most harm was done by the Saturday lunchtime previews – *On the Ball* on ITV and Sam Leitch's slot in *Grandstand*.

These programmes were extremely well done. They were full of interviews, analysis of previous matches, snatches from the top Continental and world matches, and discussions between players and managers. I could imagine thousands of people sitting down at 12.50 to watch and then saying: 'Oh well, the weather doesn't look too good today. Let's stay at home and watch the rugby on the box.'

These programmes lost their impact as a trailer, presented in such a way that people interested in football would say to themselves 'I must go and see that match now' because they finished so close to kick-off time. Anyone living a few miles from his local ground would find difficulty in getting to the match after watching them, especially if a big crowd was expected.

The time to show the football previews should be on Friday

nights, say at 10.30. Shown then, they would have a far better chance of whetting the appetite.

I have already given my views about play-backs on TV. I do not see why TV evidence should be admitted at FA Disciplinary hearings. And after the Ernie Machin case, when a player successfully challenged a FA punishment in the High Court on the strength of film evidence, I think the FA might have agreed.

Whatever the TV cameras showed would never affect the referee's decision. Usually the cameras would be thirty or forty yards from the incident, sometimes much more; and the angle could be different.

A shot from a camera placed on the touchline can suggest that a ball is over the goal line. But you can only tell when the ball is over the line if the camera is on the line itself – in the position of the linesman.

There was a controversy about a goal in the Crystal Palace v Arsenal First Division match at Selhurst Park in 1972. Charlie George took a penalty and Palace's young reserve goalkeeper Paul Hammond pushed the ball on to the post and it rebounded, ran off his back and over the line where Hammond grabbed it and pulled it back.

The linesman signalled a goal and the referee pointed to the centre. But the Palace players – usually among the best behaved when it comes to protests – argued that it hadn't gone over.

The ITV cameras showed that incident over and over again on the Sunday afternoon 'Big Match' programme, but they couldn't prove whether it was over the line or not because their camera was at a wrong angle.

There was also a controversy about an alleged offside goal that match, but with the camera not being level with the Arsenal player when the ball was last kicked, it was impossible for the film to prove anything.

This is where I think the use of TV film is grossly unfair. And not only because it is denied to Third and Fourth Division players. You would need cameras all the way round the ground to be fair to everyone, and that would cost thousands of pounds. It is an expensive business filming a football match with the normal three cameras let alone scores of them.

A tackle may look entirely different to the referee who is

142

standing on one side, than it does to the TV camera on the other side. The referee has the advantage of being able to see the intent – the expression on the player's face. He can hear the comments made.

He also knows what has happened previously. Whether the guilty player has been chopped down himself earlier in the match, and this is his way of retaliating. This is rarely shown on TV because only forty-five minutes of action is allowed to be shown out of the ninety minutes' play.

The Ernie Machin case was thoroughly bad for football, however strongly Coventry Football Club might have felt that Machin was innocent of his alleged offence against Wyn Davies, the Welsh international centre-forward. The High Court verdict meant that any club which thought one of its players was wrongly dealt with in an FA Court could engage a team of lawyers and fight an appeal in the civil law court.

Machin was sent off by Manchester referee Ricky Nicholson for fouling Newcastle's Wyn Davies in a League game in 1970. He appealed to the FA Disciplinary Committee and lost. Derrick Robins, the millionaire chairman of Coventry, decided to make a test case in the High Court because he felt Machin was innocent.

The case was heard before Mr Justice Bristow in October 1972. After seeing the TV evidence, the Judge decreed that the Disciplinary Committee's decision to uphold Machin's sending off was wrong. He ordered that Machin's £50 and £43 costs of the committee hearing should be returned to him and the three-week ban suspended.

'The TV film showed conclusively that the referee's version was quite inconsistent with the facts,' said the Judge. 'No reasonable tribunal would have reached the conclusion that the facts alleged in the referee's report were proved.'

The Judge went on to say that the referee's report was that Wyn Davies got up and after both he and Machin had fallen and that Machin while lying on the ground, kicked him just below the knee. But the film showed Machin was in possession of the ball and tried unsuccessfully to get it past Wyn Davies. It bounced off Davies's leg. He turned towards the ball and Machin then performed what might have been a tackle intending to play the ball, or a tackle intending to play the man.

143

The Judge added that although the Committee had agreed that the referee's report did not tally with the film, they still convicted Machin.

'It would be difficult to find a clearer example of the committee failing to conduct this hearing in accordance with the rules of natural justice,' he said.

The FA were most aggrieved at this decision. Mr Stokes said he thought the Committee would ban TV evidence in future. Cliff Lloyd said he did not expect a flood of High Court actions to follow.

'The FA now have an appeals procedure to an independent tribunal,' he said. 'Unfortunately there was none at the time. We were compelled to go to law.'

He said the PFA would resist another ban on the use of TV evidence. 'If this happens, we will do everything we can to resist it. If the FA changed the rules now because of this case, it would be a terrible thing to do. If TV exposes a mistake, that is not something they can hide. Anyone sitting in judgement must be sure of being right before handing out penalties.'

I sympathized with the referee, Mr Nicholson. He thought referees were asked to put too many facts in their reports. 'We should simply have stated what the offence was, and then have had the chance to see TV, like the player, before giving evidence. No one can remember every second of ninety minutes' play. And very good advocates like Cliff Lloyd will always be able to pick holes in detailed reports. Having seen the film again, I believe it still reinforces what I did.'

After the case, Bernard Joy, the football correspondent of the *Evening Standard*, called me to ask my views. I told him: 'The referee's decision is right. It's got to be right, and no playback on TV can convince him otherwise because at the time it was right.'

I was speaking in my capacity as President of the Association of Football League Referees and Linesmen. Joy wrote that the referee must remain the ultimate authority on the field. The alternative is anarchy, he said. Joy has criticized me in the past but I must say I agreed with him there.

Later that week, the Football League asked Jimmy Hill for his views on the controversies in the Arsenal v Palace match in case the London Weekend presentation of the match contravened the League's agreement with the TV companies about not pillorying referees.

Hill told them: 'There is no question of the referee being pilloried. Crystal Palace criticized the referee, Harry New, and so did most of the journalists. In fact, the fairest showing he had was on TV. The camera proved nothing except to emphasize the referee's difficulties in making a split-second decision. It is as impossible for a camera in the middle of the stand as it is for a person sitting there, to judge hairline decisions on the goal line.'

I didn't see the programme so had no idea how Hill treated the subject. But I had seen several incidents where the playbacks were used to show that a referee might have made a mistake. This undermines the authority of the referee, which shouldn't be allowed to happen. Players talk about incidents. The next match the referee takes, his control over players may be weakened because of something shown on TV the week before.

Alan Hardaker criticized the Machin verdict:

What would happen today if we had a goal-over-the-line incident such as that in the 1932 Cup Final which enabled Newcastle to beat Arsenal? Would Arsenal demand that the match be replayed?

The next thing will be for a batsman in a Test match to demand a replay because cameras proved he was wrongly given out. When lawyers come into the game they are a cancer. The referee's decision on the field must be accepted as right, even though he is human and makes mistakes.

TV producers are to blame. They are looking for a gimmick because it is a show, not a report of a match. They project themselves, the programme and the company, and football itself is relegated to rank of the chorus.

Football only reflects the age in querying decisions. Unions have arbitrators but they don't accept their decisions unless it suits them.

I have been pilloried myself because the League have considered censoring TV. But we cannot tolerate the pillorying of match officials who are unable to defend themselves.

Most referees tended to agree with Hardaker. We were un-

145

happy about TV play-backs at this time. We felt the referee should be the only judge – not the High Court Judge. Once the referee had given his decision, it was up to the FA Disciplinary Committee to uphold it or confirm that it was right but award no penalty against the player if there were redeeming circumstances.

Once the High Court can intervene in sporting matters, sport will no longer be sport as we know it. The prizes will go to the richest clubs, who hire the best lawyers.

I have nothing against televising soccer. I just think the FA should ban the use of filmed evidence at their hearings. It has got them into a lot of bother.

The interests of justice were not better served by having film evidence. It merely meant that there was one law for the rich and another for the poor, and that can't be fair, surely? I never encountered a Fourth Division player who used film evidence at a hearing. Yet there are more Fourth Division than First Division clubs.

14

Benfica

The ball hit the Ajax player on the arm inside the penalty area
but I didn't think he handled deliberately. So I waved play on
and the 70,000 crowd in the Stadium of Light, Lisbon,
erupted.

Hundreds of bottles, cushions, oranges and lemons were
thrown on the pitch. How dare this English referee stop Benfica
having a penalty! Fans tried to rush on to the pitch but were
held back by police.

But one gentleman did get on the field and made for me . . .
a policeman. As he waved his baton angrily he shouted, 'Hand
ball!'

I said, 'Whose side are you on?' The irate policeman was
held back by some of his colleagues and the groundstaff
started clearing the pitch of missiles.

The match was Benfica v Ajax in the European Cup on 19
April 1972. It was one of the trickiest matches of the many I
had abroad. Ajax won the first leg 1–0 in Amsterdam, and
tickets for the second leg were sold out weeks in advance.

The atmosphere in the Stadium of Light that night was the
most overwhelming I encountered anywhere. The noise hit you
when you walked up the steps from the underground dressing-
rooms.

Everyone present wanted Benfica to win. No English crowd
can compare with a Benfica crowd on such an occasion. Ajax
started well and scored an early goal which I disallowed
because I thought the scorer held off one of the Benfica players.

147

I saw the match later on TV and it didn't show the incident.

It was a tight match. Ajax, despite their reputation for attacking football, played defensively and as the minutes went by the Benfica players and supporters became more frustrated.

Every time the ball went out of play it would be lobbed back immediately by the scores of youngsters who were acting as ball boys. If the ball went quite a distance the boys didn't bother to get it. They promptly threw in another ball to save time. This was against the laws. I kept trying to insist on having the original ball fetched back but it was soon lost. The crowd kept whistling. I would be highly unpopular if I stuck to my point so I relented.

But I reported this breach of regulations to UEFA and Benfica were later fined a nominal sum. Saving time didn't help Benfica because the match ended in a 0–0 draw and they were out of the competition.

International referees are paid precisely nothing for refereeing European and international matches. They get only the FIFA allowance of 80 Swiss francs a day spending money. But the practice on the Continent is for the clubs taking part in European matches to give the referee and linesmen lavish presents.

In some quarters this might be looked on as a form of bribery, but it isn't. Clubs like Benfica are extremely generous. They usually give the opposing players and officials presents too.

After that Benfica v Ajax match I received a 19-carat gold whistle and a brooch. No one could say that the thought of receiving these presents had affected my performance, especially after disallowing that appeal for a penalty!

I received a total of seven watches during my time as an international referee in Europe, some of them gold. Even behind the Iron Curtain, clubs are generous with presents. I received a valuable glass vase in Poland once. In Belgium I was given an electric razor.

Whenever I did a foreign match on my own I would usually take out some English glassware with me to give to my linesmen who came from another country. Giving presents is traditional on the Continent. It doesn't mean that the clubs are trying to buy your integrity. It is merely something that has always happened and no doubt will continue to happen.

English clubs give presents too, but usually pennants and much less expensive souvenirs. I never had a conscience about accepting presents – not even a silver casket from one club which I later found was worth more than I would earn in a week – because I was not being paid. Usually I had given up four days' work to make the trip. I looked on presents as perks.

My first visit to Benfica was on 24 February 1965, when I was a linesman. Kevin Howley was the referee. The match was against Real Madrid. What a game that was! There were many great players on the field – di Stefano, Puskas, Gento, Mario Coluna and Eusebio among them.

Puskas wasn't very happy with Kevin Howley. He thought he hadn't given him anything – as if referees are in the habit of giving decisions for players!

Kevin Howley had his whistle on a long piece of rope so that he could twirl it round at the end of the game if spectators came near him. But there were no riots that night.

My final contact with Benfica was the unhappiest of the lot – a friendly at Highbury in 1971. Arsenal won 6–2. Although it was supposed to be a friendly, it was a hard match to handle.

The Benfica team lost their heads when George Graham scored in the seventy-seventh minute. They thought he was off-side but I was in a good position to see that he wasn't, and the linesman didn't flag. The whole Benfica team mobbed me, with the exception of the goalkeeper.

Not being able to speak the language of the players is usually an advantage in these games with foreign sides. You can make yourself understood more plainly with gestures. There was no doubting what Eusebio and company were saying.

Some players grabbed my arms, pulled my shirt and pushed me. One spat in my face. It was impossible to caution any particular player or send one off because the whole team seemed involved. If one went, the whole lot would have had to go.

It was four minutes before we were able to control the Portuguese players. Normally Portuguese footballers are most disciplined but when they go, they really go! I reported the whole team to UEFA with the exception of the goalkeeper.

My report was forwarded to the Portuguese FA but I never heard what became of it.

Afterwards Eusebio said: 'The man in black was the best English player. He did not do the job properly. English referees are usually very good. Not this one.'

Jimmy Hagan, the Englishman who was managing Benfica at the time said: 'I am fully aware that we are being reported to the FA. But had there been FA men here they would have seen for themselves. I warned my boys before the start that we might be up against it. I know Burtenshaw. We all know Burtenshaw. It was an open incident for all to see. We have always had a high regard for English referees but I think our opinions have altered.' Now for the crunch bit which condemns his own club. 'My players were incensed but I do not condone their actions. I gave them a talking-to afterwards. Right or wrong, they must accept the referee's decision.'

Benfica were far from happy when I was chosen to do the Ajax match the following year. When I asked for the ball as a souvenir, Hagan brought an old ball in. But so many balls had been used, perhaps it was a pointless request to make!

The only time I was physically attacked by a player was at the Lierse SK v PSV Eindhoven UEFA Cup match in Belgium on 8 December 1971. The player was a Yugoslav, Radovic Lazar. There was nothing controversial in the match except for a disallowed appeal for a penalty. I didn't remember having much trouble with any of the players.

At the end of the game I waited with my linesmen for the players to leave the field. When the players had all gone into the tunnel, we followed. Waiting at the end of the tunnel was a player I didn't recognize. He struck me in the face, grabbed my shirt and pulled me towards him. One of the linesmen tried to pull him away and was kicked in the leg. Other officials near-by came to our assistance and the player was dragged off.

Later I went to the Eindhoven dressing-room to find out the identity of the player concerned. I saw him but he refused to give me his number and had to be held back by his team-mates.

I had to get his number from an Eindhoven official before I could make out my report. Later I was at a reception when I saw the player again. I was rather apprehensive. But he came over and apologized for his behaviour through an interpreter. I felt sorry for him. He had simply lost his head. Over what, I never knew. UEFA later suspended him from taking part in European matches for three years.

Although the standard of living is lower behind the Iron Curtain, referees are looked after very well. When I arrived in Warsaw for a match I was presented with a bunch of flowers at the airport.

That evening I was in my hotel bedroom when there was a knock at the door. I said 'Come in' and a girl entered and said, 'Mr Burtenshaw, the referee from England? I have come to spend some time with you.' I didn't know quite what to make of that! She spoke good English. I gave her some English cigarettes and she left.

Continental clubs make a habit of entertaining the referee before and after the match. I remember one memorable evening at a night club in Milan paid for by the Inter club. The gate for the match – against a Czech club – was only 3,000. Ridiculous in a stadium the size of the San Siro, which has a capacity of 80,000.

Our party probably spent a good part of the receipts at the night club afterwards. When I left at about three in the morning the bill was over the £100 mark.

Each country in membership with FIFA has seven referees on the FIFA panel. That means that a country like Zambia, which has a total of forty referees, nearly all in the beginners' stage, can have the same representation as England, which has 30,000.

I was appointed to the international list in 1965. It is a high point in one's career. It means that you are one of the top referees in the country and are looked on as one of the best in the world.

I was working in my shop one day five years later when a reporter from a London evening newspaper rang and said, 'What do you think about being removed from the FIFA list?'

I told him I didn't know I had been removed. He said it was true. It had just come over the ticker tapes. I was shattered. I couldn't say anything. When another reporter rang I said 'It was like having my legs cut off'.

I put my coat on and started walking up the road. I walked

and walked. I must have been out for four hours and covered nearly twenty miles when I suddenly felt so tired that I rang Dorothy and said, 'Come and collect me.'

So many things went through my mind. Why had they done it? What had I done wrong? Would I lose my chance of doing the Cup Final? I knew I had not been refereeing well in some recent matches, but abroad I thought I was up to my usual standard.

It was like someone telling Bobby Moore he would never play for England again. There was no reason. Officially I had been told nothing. But I knew it must be right.

Shortly afterwards I had to go to the annual conference of referees. I didn't feel like going but had to. No one wanted to speak to me. They didn't know what to say. It was almost unheard-of for a top referee to be removed from the FIFA list.

I saw Mr McMullen there and asked him why I had been left off the list. 'Your refereeing has gone off,' he said.

Denis Follows told me not to be too despondent. I said I would do all I could to prove his committee wrong. The FA Referees' Committee had made the recommendation to FIFA. Now I had to show them I could still do it.

Right after I first received the news I came home and got all my papers, records and medals out and threw them in the dustbin ... I was so disgusted. Luckily, Dorothy rescued most of them and hid them, including £200 of Premium Bonds which I had inadvertently tossed out in my rage!

I decided I would carry on. I worked out a new training schedule and at the start of the following season felt fitter than I had ever been. I straightened myself out. Perhaps the Committee had been right. Perhaps my work had deteriorated.

The early matches of that season went so well that people used to come up to me and say: 'Are you still refereeing? We don't hear so much about you these days.'

That was the finest compliment I could get. It meant that I was doing my job, I had a succession of excellent reports from Assessors. I felt that I had got it right again. Near the end of the season I was given the FA Cup Final. And at the end, I heard I was back on FIFA.

One of the most pleasant things about being an international referee is the foreign lecture tour. I made several of these and enjoyed every moment of them. In 1968 Sir Stanley Rous, President of FIFA, recommended me for an assignment in Zambia. I was then working as a telephonist at the GPO in Yarmouth. I applied for time off but was refused. I decided to go anyway, even though I was not being paid for going.

I was already in the departure lounge at London Airport when I rang the Norwich Traffic officer and he said that I could go without pay. It was because of this kind of difficulty in getting time off that I finally left my job and bought a shop so that I could be my own boss.

I had a good time in Zambia, journeying round the country in a succession of cars which kept breaking down. Petrol was on the black market and I had to buy most of it myself out of my daily allowance from the British Council, which was sponsoring my trip. I also had to send money home to Dorothy to keep the house and family going.

Leicester City were touring Zambia at the time and I refereed three of their matches. In one game at Lusaka, against the national side, their centre-forward Frank Large charged the goalkeeper and the crowd started demonstrating. Later a Zambian player kicked a Leicester forward and should really have gone off, but by that time stones and missiles had descended all around us and I told Dave Gibson, the Leicester player, 'If I send anyone off, we'll never get off the pitch.'

It was the one occasion when I didn't do my duty according to the laws of the game.

Frank Large didn't know it at the time, but he had been sold to Fulham while he was away. Allan Clarke went to Leicester in an exchange deal and Fulham also received a large cash payment. At the end of the game the goalie who had been injured in the crash with Large walked off to hospital. No one bothered about him.

Leicester were due to play another match in Livingstone and I was again supposed to be the referee, but the Zambians refused to have me. The Leicester officials told them: 'Either Mr Burtenshaw referees this game or we don't play it.' The Zambians conceded the point. We flew to Livingstone in a rickety old Dakota, with me acting as the unofficial barman.

Neither side remembered to bring a ball. So just before the match was due to start, with the ground full of spectators, we discovered there was no ball in the stadium! An official scooted up the road to another ground where two police teams were playing and brought their match to a sudden end by demanding the ball.

It was an old, bladder-type ball, and I told Leicester goalkeeper Peter Shilton, 'For goodness sake don't kick it too hard, you'll burst it.' The crowd were unhappy about the delayed start but Dave Gibson kept them in good humour with a ball-juggling act.

I was due to travel up-country for another lecture but the trip was put off when someone sent me a cutting from a local newspaper. A gentleman had written a letter to the newspaper saying that he was going to shoot me when I came to town. The British Council told me I could cancel the trip and I did. If newspapers could publish letters like that, there was a fair chance the fellow wasn't joking!

In 1969 I went to North America to referee some matches in the new soccer League there. This was another enjoyable trip and I went to places like Dallas, Philadelphia, Baltimore, Kansas, Houston and Washington. The teams taking part were mainly from England and Scotland – West Ham, Wolves, Kilmarnock and Aston Villa among them.

In one match, Bobby Moore put through his own goal but the spectators were ignorant of the laws and didn't think that counted! The matches were played on baseball grounds. The surfaces were not very satisfactory.

I spent a lot of time lecturing. At one meeting, a parent told me: 'I'm so excited about this new game because it means my boy can play it. You don't have to be six feet four and sixteen stone to play your game.'

American football, the big sport in North America, is played almost exclusively by giants; and smaller lads, particularly the newer immigrants, have little chance of being successful in it. When we were in Atlanta I stayed at the same hotel as Aston Villa. Tommy Docherty was the Villa manager then and he caused quite a stir by fining two of his players for misconduct off the field.

My departure flight from Kansas to New York and then home to England was scheduled to leave soon after the end of one match. I told the organizers I wouldn't be able to do the game in case I missed the plane.

'That's all right,' they said. 'Do the match as long as you can and leave in the second half. We'll provide a police escort to the airport.'

And that is what happened, except that when I arrived at the airport I had to wait two hours because the plane was held up.

In 1970 I had an even more enjoyable trip to Japan with Tottenham Hotspur, organized by Leslie Taylor of Middlesex Wanderers. The hospitality was fantastic. One of the advantages of this kind of trip is that it gives a referee an opportunity to mix with players and understand their problems. Players can also understand ours. I got on well with all the Spurs players. They were a nice bunch of fellows.

The standard of Japanese football was quite high and there was great enthusiasm in the schools for the game. The players bought laughing bags which they would switch on at all kinds of embarrassing moments . . . to the annoyance of Eddie Baily, the assistant manager. The crowds were large and very excitable. They applauded everything.

I found myself in a riot during my trip to South Africa in the summer of 1972. I travelled 22,000 miles lecturing and refereeing matches, and everything was orderly until I did the Kaiser Chiefs v Orlando Pirates match in Soweto. These were the two top teams in the non-white League.

The standard of ball skills of these players was absolutely incredible. The players were all like Rodney Marsh – beating a succession of opponents with body swerves, dribbles and extravagant tricks. But the team play wasn't so good, nor was the temperament of some of the players!

The Orlando Stadium, scene of several previous incidents, was packed with 25,000 people with another 60,000 outside when I arrived. Hundreds of fans clung to the roofs of the stands. I gave a penalty against the home team which failed to enhance my popularity, but the Pirates equalized when one of their forwards beat three men and the goalkeeper and raised his arms in salute to the crowd before he put the ball into the back of the net.

The away team scored again near the end and the crowd

rioted. Stones, bottles and beer-cans were thrown on the pitch at the final whistle, and a roof collapsed. One man died in the fall and several others had to be taken to hospital. Two youths were knifed and a dozen more were bitten by police dogs or struck by missiles.

The English newspapers later reported that I had started the riot, but this wasn't true. Apparently these two teams have a record of misconduct. The Kaiser Chiefs were started as a breakaway group from the Pirates, and the Pirates have never forgiven them for it.

I hadn't wanted to do the match anyway. The day before I was suffering from the flu-bug but felt I had to go ahead because I wanted to do a game between coloured teams. Mr Vivian Granger, general manager of the National Football League, told the local newspapers that the penalty award was perfectly justified and Mr Burtenshaw had refereed magnificently. So that was one riot I couldn't be blamed for!

'The authorities have had a lot of trouble at Orlando Pirates matches,' he said. 'The supporters take defeat very badly. It is time the authorities did something about an adequate stadium at Orlando. That would rule out a lot of trouble.'

The hospitality I received from both non-white and English-speaking people in South Africa was tremendous. I think there is a big future there for football. Most of the top clubs are full of English players like Johnny Haynes and George Eastham but there is plenty of home talent being developed. It just needs organizing.

Unfortunately, the standard of refereeing, though improving rapidly, still lags behind the improvement in playing standards. I hoped that I was able to do something to help.

15

'You're a coward'

Gordon Hill did the Chelsea v Arsenal FA Cup quarter-final at Stamford Bridge on Saturday, 17 March 1973 but was in Italy for an Anglo-Italian Cup match when the replay took place at Highbury the following Tuesday. So the FA asked me to take the game. I was very excited about the prospect: it would be my last FA Cup tie.

Highbury was sure to be full. The previous Saturday 12,000 fans had paid £1.80 each to see the match on closed circuit TV in cinemas in North London because Stamford Bridge could only hold 40,000 spectators at that time. The score in the first match was 2–2. Everyone agreed it had been a fine game.

When I arrived at the Arsenal underground station two hours before Tuesday's kick off I had to fight my way out of the station and up the road. The crowd was enormous. A policeman told me: 'They'll be shutting the gates long before the start if this continues.'

It seemed that every Arsenal and Chelsea fan wanted to see this replay. The winners were drawn to meet Sunderland – a lowly second Division club – in the semi-final.

One of the first people I met at Highbury was the Arsenal left-back Bob McNab. He said he thought the winners would have a great chance of getting to Wembley. Chelsea were out of every other competition. Only the FA Cup was left. They would be sure to make a great fight of it. So would Arsenal, who were chasing the Double again.

At 6.30 I went out on to the pitch with the linesmen Jack

Griffiths and Tom Bune. The pitch looked as though it had
been heavily watered. There is nothing to stop clubs watering
the pitch if they want to. I thought it was a good idea: it is
extremely difficult to play good football on a bone hard, dry
pitch which has little grass on it.

The ground was full when I came out at 7.27. The
atmosphere was unique. The North Bank was seething with
bodies and noise. I was very tense – even the calmest of people
would have been tense in such an atmosphere.

Chelsea surprised me with the quality of their football in the
opening minutes. They had not had a particularly good season.
They'd had a lot of injuries and the team was chopped and
changed about almost every week. But now they came out and
took the game to Arsenal. Some of their moves were gems.
Peter Osgood struck some wonderful passes.

I sensed that though this match meant so much to both sides,
the players wanted to play it in the right spirit. There was no
vicious tackling. I had little to do except run as quickly as I
could. The pace was so fast that I found myself sprinting up
and down the softish pitch, grateful for any stoppages.

The first and only bad foul of the game came in the fifteenth
minute. As Bob McNab cleared the ball near the edge of the
Arsenal penalty area Chris Garland deliberately ran into him
and tripped him up. Garland's attitude was aggressive and totally unnecessary in the mood of the match. I blew at once for a
free kick and started to get my card out to caution him. But
the players had not heard the whistle. I had a good, loud
whistle that night but it would have needed a fifteen-gun salute
to stop the play above that din. McNab's clearance found Ray
Kennedy just inside the halfway line. Kennedy volleyed the
ball ahead of Charlie George and it was a chase between
George, Chelsea left-back Eddie McCreadie going one way and
goalkeeper John Phillips going the other.

As the ball bounced on the edge of the area, George headed
it on and Phillips and McCreadie crashed into each other and
fell to the ground. George ran on and thumped the ball into
the empty net. The fans were overjoyed.

They were soon quietened by the sight of me in the other
penalty area pointing for a free-kick to Arsenal. I could

158

imagine their reaction. 'What's he given now? Must be advantage! What a load of rubbish!'

But in my view there could be no advantage in a situation like this. Garland had committed a bad foul. If I had let it go the game could have turned nasty. It was just unfortunate that some of the players didn't hear the whistle.

The Arsenal players protested. Alan Ball in particular had a lot to say. So did Charlie George. Ball persisted and I had to tell him to shut his mouth. I had to allow a little leeway because of the circumstances.

I got the game going again with a free kick to Arsenal. Four minutes later Chelsea went ahead. John Hollins, playing at right-back, centred from the right, Bill Garner headed back and Peter Houseman nodded the ball past Bob Wilson at the near post. It was a deserved goal. Chelsea continued to look the better side. Their players were passing accurately and working hard. Arsenal would have to fight to stay in the match.

In the fortieth minute Arsenal winger George Armstrong was making a run on the right hand side of the pitch when Steve Kember brought him down from behind. I was in a good position – on the far side of the penalty area on the opposite diagonal to linesman Jack Griffiths. From where I stood it looked as though the incident had happened outside the penalty area. I ran over and pointed to a spot a foot or two outside the area. Immediately I was besieged with angry Arsenal players – Alan Ball, Eddie Kelly, Pat Rice, George Armstrong and Ray Kennedy.

Armstrong claimed that he was inside the area when felled; skipper Frank McLintock implored me to consult the linesman; they were all very heated – shouting and gesticulating. But I was firm in my decision because I thought I was right. McLintock ran over to the linesman to protest with some other players. He told Jack Griffiths that as the linesman he knew it was a penalty and should have signalled. Mr Griffiths replied that it wasn't his decision: it was the referee's prerogative. McLintock told him he was much nearer than the referee. 'You ought to tell him', he said.

McLintock said later the linesman seemed to be nodding his head as though in agreement. 'I went back to the referee and told him the linesman said it was a penalty', McLintock told the reporters 'I said the linesman wanted to speak to him'.

In effect, I was conned. The linesman had not said he wanted to see me. But I went to Jack Griffiths just the same. Three Arsenal players went with me. I turned and ordered them away. I didn't want them listening or trying to influence our decision.

Jack, who had just become a JP in Oxford, was only thirteen yards from the incident whereas I was forty yards away. I said to him: 'I have given a free kick just outside the box. I am right.'

Jack Griffiths is one of the best linesmen in the country and a very honest man. 'No, it was inside the box, Norman', he said. 'And it was a penalty.'

I asked him if he was sure and he said he was. Next day when I saw the re-run of the TV film at ITN you could pick up the conversation from our lip movements.

I had spoken to Jack in such a way that he could have accepted what I told him. But he was strong-minded enough to give me his honest and entirely opposite opinion.

Why should I have consulted him now, after protests, and not before if there was some doubt? The answer is that at first there was no doubt in my mind: I thought I was right. But the Arsenal players were *so* insistent that I began to think that perhaps I might have been wrong. Normally I ignored protests of this sort as the Arsenal players knew only too well. But this was an entirely new situation and I thought it was only fair to see the linesman.

The ultimate decision rested with me. I could stick to my first decision or change it. In my eleven years on the League list I could never remember changing a decision, but I did now. I pointed to the penalty spot. Now it was the turn of the Chelsea players to be incensed. Some of them started to take the mickey out of me.

'Which way is it?' said one. 'Sure it's not a corner?' asked another. Peter Osgood told some reporters later that he called me a coward for listening to the Arsenal protests. 'It was the first time I have seen this referee change his mind', he said. 'I told him he was a coward.'

I did not hear him say that. Osgood subsequently denied saying these words but the FA called for an investigation.

McCreadie and Kember were particularly angry. Kember said: 'I thought you were the referee who was always right. You're not right any more.'

Then he pushed his finger into the side of his head as if to signify that I was a nut case. I could understand the frustrations of the players – Chelsea's and Arsenal's. I would probably have reacted in the same way myself. It was because I understood their feelings that I didn't caution anyone.

John Dempsey, the Chelsea centre-half, was very upset and had a lot to say. But his goalkeeper, John Phillips came up and put his hand over his mouth – a very sensible move, I thought.

Alan Ball placed the ball on the penalty spot and hit it against the stanchion on Phillips's right side for the equalizer. As I turned towards the centre of the field, some of the Chelsea players were still shouting. I made a wide detour of Dempsey, who was standing in my path. I didn't want to get involved in any more rows.

The linesman was criticized for his part in the affair because he didn't signal that it was a penalty. But since I had already made my decision he didn't have to signal: Jack Griffiths acted quite properly.

Experiments have been made with a flag-across-the-chest signal when a linesman thinks there is a penalty but I am against too many signals. The present system seems perfectly adequate; it may have fallen down in this instance but it was the first time in eleven years that it had produced this kind of controversy.

The important thing was that the right decision had been made in the end, even if I had to change my mind. I admit I made an error of judgement. I am human, after all, just like the players.

In a high-pressure match like this you have no time to think about decisions: you have to make your mind up quickly. Just before the first half finished, Charlie George jumped to a right-wing cross and fisted the ball into the net. Thousands of Arsenal fans must have thought it was a goal because they roared with delight. George leapt in the air and saluted the 'goal'. So did another Arsenal player.

What the hell, I thought. Who are they trying to kid? Fortunately I was in a good position, almost exactly the same

161

M

position as I was for the Francis Lee goal at Tottenham Hotspur. But this time I saw the incident clearly and blew for a free kick to Chelsea.

George's attitude angered me. Why did he have to pretend he had scored a goal? What if I hadn't seen it? We would have been in another row. There are enough pressures on the referee without this kind of thing happening.

As we came off for half-time I felt very depressed. I was troubled by the penalty incident. I thought I was having a good match yet that would be ignored. People would concentrate on my one mistake.

I didn't say a word in the dressing room for several minutes. Tom Bune diplomatically went to the toilet. When he came back, I said: 'We haven't got to let that incident affect us. We've got to go out there and continue to do a good job.'

I couldn't remember being so keyed up and tense before. In the second half I had to keep telling myself to forget the incident. But it weighed on my mind.

The pace of the game was still very fast. By the end I felt physically tired. I thought: 'If there's extra time I'll have a heart attack!' I couldn't recall running so hard before.

There was a minor incident when Osgood and Ball clashed fleetingly. They saw me looking towards them and broke it off.

As Ball ran by I said: 'I can remember the time when you would have had a go.'

He replied: 'But you were watching Norman.' I thought that was a pleasant change from his tone earlier in the match!

Arsenal's winning goal came in the fifty-eighth minute. McNab crossed from the right and Kennedy headed in at the far post. I was well positioned to see that there was no infringement; there were no arguments.

In the final minutes Kennedy was three times through but each time Phillips prevented him from scoring with splendid saves. The last time I held my head, I was so surprised that Phillips had been able to thwart him.

There was practically no time to add on for injuries. When I blew the final whistle I made sure I was on the far side away from the tunnel. I didn't want the players to pass me. The Chelsea players were still giving me black looks!

McLintock came up and started to put his arm round me. I

said: 'Get away from me.' That may have sounded rude but I was very worked up and didn't want to be congratulated as if I was doing more than my job.

'What does that mean?' he said.

'It means I don't want you near me,' I said.

I was in a very tense state. John Hollins came up and shook hands. I thought that was a more appropriate gesture than embracing the referee. I reflected on what a sporting, open match it had been. If only that penalty incident hadn't happened!

When I arrived at my dressing room I told the official outside that I didn't want anyone to come in for twenty minutes. I felt I had to have a chance to cool down. Later Ken Aston from the FIFA Referees' Committee came in to congratulate me. He thought it had been the best game he had seen all season. A chap from the New Zealand FA also said what a magnificent game it was. It hadn't occurred to me that it was as good as all that. I was too absorbed in it. The penalty affair apart, it had been a fine match to handle. It was a good FA Cup tie to go out on. I would never take another one.

It was nearly an hour before we left Highbury – the two linesmen and I and five friends from the refereeing world. We had quite a long walk to one of the cars. There were few fans about. But at one street corner a group of about a dozen Chelsea fans recognized me and started to shout abuse. They began walking after me. If I had been alone it could have been a nasty situation but there were eight of us and one or two were pretty big fellows.

We called at a pub for a drink. I couldn't remember being so tired and mentally drained after a match. Though the pub was miles away at Euston it was filled with football fans who had been at Highbury.

I was soon recognized. 'Good old Norman,' they sang. That was a relief. They were Arsenal fans. 'Thanks for the penalty', said one.

I held my glass up. 'What are you having?' the fellow said. I said half of bitter but my friends would probably like something stronger. We had a convivial few minutes before the eleven o'clock closing time.

Next day I was invited to the ITN studios near the Post Office Tower to be interviewed by Robert Kee about the penalty. Lots of people had said to me they had seen the film on the previous night's news. When I saw it I was amazed. Armstrong was inside the box all the time. He must have been a yard or two from the line when he was brought down. It was staggering: the view from the other side of the penalty area had been completely different. I was very relieved that I had spoken to the linesman.

Mr Kee asked me if I thought I was encouraging players to argue by accepting their pleas to see the linesman. It was a tricky question; perhaps I was, but this was an isolated case and had only happened once in my career. The film proved that the linesman was right; I would have been made to look an idiot if I had stuck to my original decision.

I had applied the eighteenth and unwritten law – common-sense: in the circumstances it seemed the common-sense thing to see Jack Griffiths even though I had been sure in my own mind that I was right.

16
Life at the bottom

Football fans think of the game in terms of 50,000 crowds, £100,000 players, *Match of the Day* and £1,000 a man if you get to Wembley. But the Football League is not all like that. Most of the member clubs are so broke that the manager has to watch how many long-distance telephone calls he makes. There are more clubs with gates under 5,000 than there are clubs with gates over 50,000.

In my travels to these smaller clubs – and I have been to most of them – I found that the hospitality and friendliness usually surpassed that of most of the rich clubs. Out on the field, the players were more honest. They didn't feign injury or cheat. Perhaps they are luckier than the men at the top. The pressure of winning at all costs is not so heavy on them. The only pressure they have is staying in a job.

Hartlepool of the Fourth Division were one of my favourite clubs. In 1955 their Victoria Ground once held 17,000 fans, but it sees nothing like that now. But they are a friendly lot all the same. I remember after one match – tired after the 300-mile drive there and doing the game – I was soaking in the bath when an official came in and asked if there was anything I wanted.

'Yes,' I said. 'There's a bit of a problem here. How do I get the water out of the bath? The plug won't come out.'

The official pointed to a nail hanging on a piece of string on the wall. 'We use that four-inch nail,' he said. You couldn't imagine that happening at the marble halls of Highbury!

165

Hartlepool are one of the few clubs that send Christmas cards to the referees and all the other clubs in the League. The card is full of Shakespearean quotations.

The longest trip I had to make from my Great Yarmouth home was to Torquay and Plymouth, 323 miles each way. My wife was ill just before Easter one year, and the Football League asked me if I would like to take her for a few days to Devon and do a couple of matches. I thought it was a kind gesture by the League.

Gililngham in Kent are a hospitable club. Their chairman, Dr Grossmark, always used to take the referee out to lunch. I think he realized that the ground was some way out of town and there were no facilities for eating.

Colchester, another Fourth Division club, are my nearest League club except for Ipswich and Norwich, which I rarely did for obvious reasons. Colchester are another friendly club, but you have to be careful you don't bang your head on a girder when leaving.

Even the top referees in the country – the seven on the FIFA international list – have to do their share of smaller games. I reckoned I did about thirty-five matches a season on average, covering anything up to 30,000 miles a year. Roughly half of these were First Division.

Most of the funniest things happened in the Third and Fourth Divisions. Once I decided to call a match off at Peterborough because of ice. Discretion in these matters is always left to the referee. The officials of the two clubs may try to influence the referee but he shouldn't take any notice.

The Peterborough manager was so angry with my decision that he promptly arranged for a friendly match to take place at the scheduled time! He was reprimanded by the Football Association.

At another match, at Scunthorpe, there was thick fog but I decided to take a chance. Ron Ashman, whom I used to know at Norwich was the manager and he had several former Norwich players in his side.

Leaving the ground afterwards, the fog thickened and I was last seen driving down the wrong side of a dual carriageway! I had to abandon the car and stay the night.

One club I wasn't so keen on going to was Reading, because

some years ago their secretary, Fred May, queried my expenses. An unheard-of thing! The home club always pays the referee his expenses and are reimbursed by the Football League.

A match at Tranmere was postponed once because water was running down the middle. Dave Russell, the general manager, said a river ran at the bottom of the ground.

'It looks as though it's running down the pitch,' I said. A referee has to use his common-sense about these things. If he thinks there is any danger to the players he must take no chances. Tranmere, incidentally, have a wonderful set-up for a Third Division club.

At Swindon one year half the pitch was soft and the other half was hard and frozen under the stand. I decided we could play, but thought it wise to tell the players in advance because those on the soft side would probably like to wear studs and those on the icy side rubbers.

So to save the players having to come back off the pitch after the tossing of the coin to change their boots, I tossed up in the dressing-room. We went through another tossing-up ceremony on the pitch but only to keep the crowd happy.

One year it was very wet in the Midlands when I was scheduled to do a match at the Baseball ground between Derby and Nottingham Forest.

I was staying at the Midland Hotel near the station on the Friday night. Brian Clough and the Derby team were also staying there. We had a few drinks and a chat. Clough thought there was an even chance of the game taking place. I guessed if he thought that, then there was little chance.

We agreed we would go down to the ground together at ten in the morning. But I got up early and went down at nine-thirty. I didn't think it wise to make an inspection with a manager who might want the game to go on irrespective of the conditions. The Baseball Ground is not one of the best playing surfaces in the League.

I told the secretary that the match was off, and was sitting talking to him in his office when Clough rang. The secretary told him it was off. 'Put him on to me,' said Clough.

'I thought we were going down together?' he said.

'Yes, but I thought I'd see what it was like early,' I replied.

'They're playing at Wolverhampton, you know,' said Clough.

I replied, 'I don't care what they are doing at Wolverhampton, they're not playing here.' We all had a laugh.

Orient have a peculiar spot on their Brisbane Road pitch. I don't know if a doodle-bug landed there in the last war but it is a big patch which gets like a bog. You have to make a detour round it. I always warn new referees about it.

Shrewsbury's Gay Meadow always reminds me of a funny incident. I did a match there against QPR once, and as I came out a fan walked up to me and said; 'Mr Burtenshaw?'

I said 'Yes'. He held out a penny and dropped it. 'Here, that's all you're worth,' he said, and walked off.

When you have been eleven years on the list you see different faces, particularly among managers. The Notts County secretary, Mr Heath, once told me he had seen thirteen managers in his time at the club. Being a manager is the last job I would ever want in football. It is worse than being a referee!

Luton's Kenilworth Road was my least-liked ground. I had my worst-ever performance there in a match against Bournemouth. I don't know what it was. The game just got away from me. The harder I tried, the worse I became. I can understand how players have off-days. Referees are the same. What made it bad for me was that Mr McMullen, chairman of the FA Referees' Committee, was there that day.

In another match at Luton, against an Italian Under-23 side, I tore an Achilles tendon and was off for six weeks.

Are the small clubs essential to the future well-being of the Football League? I think they are. They are not so distant and remote as the big clubs. There is a more cordial atmosphere. You get to know people.

But the Football League doesn't exist on cordiality. Nor does it continue by the rich subsidizing the poor. The game is all about money, and the big clubs are so intent on getting to the top themselves that they cannot spend time and energy on supporting those below them.

Some of the new competitions, such as the Watney Cup, have brought more money in lower down. Colchester, in particular, did well out of the Watney Cup.

But clubs cannot survive on gates of 2–3,000. I think the small clubs will have to function part-time and the Divisions be regionalized to save travelling expenses.

Wages are so low in the Fourth Division – many players are earning under £40 a week – that when you referee their matches you get the impression that the win bonus of £4, or whatever it is, is vital to the players to enable them to live.

There is a better spirit among the players. There is less dissent. I don't think the Fourth Division full-back tries deliberately to maim his opponent. I never believed a First Division full-back did either, but several times I have had this kind of conversation with a First Division player:

'Come on, ref! Get hold of it. He kicked him deliberately.'

Burtenshaw: 'You mean to tell me that that player deliberately kicked a fellow player in the head because he intended to hurt him and put him out of the game.'

Player: 'Yes of course. Send him off.'

Perhaps I should have inspected his boots to see if he had any four-inch nails there!

17
The future

A few years ago a lot of referees were schoolteachers, like the former World Cup referee Ken Aston. But as the number of matches increased, so schoolteachers were unable to get sufficient time off. Most of today's referees are self-employed like me, or work in jobs where it is easy to get several days leave whenever it is wanted.

Two words which antagonize referees more than any others are 'professional referees'. People in the game are always talking about 'professional referees'. We already have them – poorly-paid professional referees.

Any person who spends half Friday travelling to a match, all day Saturday in the town where the match is being played, and most of Saturday evening and often Sunday morning returning home, is a professional. Most weeks the referee has a midweek engagement which takes another two days out of his working week. Add the time he takes to do his training, and you can see that the modern referee puts in as much time on the job as the professional player.

Only he is grossly underpaid in comparison. The amount of time the referee is involved in refereeing and the pressures surrounding the job have both increased greatly in the last decade.

Instead of the phrase 'professional referees' the words 'full-time referees' should be used. I think we are soon reaching the stage where the Football League will realize that refereeing is a full-time job. If the top referees today were asked whether they were in favour of full-time referees I think three-quarters of them would say 'Yes, provided the money was good enough'.

A contract for three years could be offered the top twenty referees, who would handle the toughest matches each week. The League know who the top twenty are, and it is most unlikely that the League would be put in a position where they would have to sack one of them before his contract expired.

This security would ease the mental pressures on referees. Even the top referees have to wait until just before the start of the following season to know if they are to be retained on the League list. But a three-year contract would guarantee some sort of future. I believe the professional managers like Don Revie who object to the so-called 'amateur' referees would welcome such a scheme.

It is often said that no referee earning, say, £3,000 or more from his normal job would give that up to become a full-time referee. I do not think the average referee has to give his job up. He can be like those players who have two jobs – football and a business outside the game.

The élite of full-time referees would have more time to train and lecture. One of the criticisms of the referee at present is that he is not physically fit. Tommy Docherty said recently he thought a quarter of the referees on the League list are unfit.

I do not think this is true. I think referees today are fitter than they have ever been. They have to be, because the pace of the game is quicker today. The days of the walking referee are over.

Retired referees like Reg Leafe, Leo Callaghan and Ken Dagnall never seemed to get above a slow trot. But they were always in control of their matches. Control is the operative word in refereeing, more so than fitness. Of course if the referee is forty yards away from an incident he is in no position to assess it properly. But these referees never found themselves in that position because of the experience which they picked up over a long hard haul to the top. It is not a question of running flat out all over the pitch, but of knowing where to run at the right time.

Reg Leafe appeared to stroll around but he was one of the finest referees ever produced in this country. Younger referees today have to be faster simply because the pressures are different than they used to be in Reg Leafe's day. Referees weren't mobbed and screamed at fifteen years ago. No one threw the ball at them or tried to tug their shirt off.

A heightened state of mental fitness is needed to cope with these additional problems. The referee of today needs to be a man of character.

Having said that our referees are fitter now than ever before, I still think there is room for improvement. The Dutch are more advanced than we are at seeing their referees are physically fit. Referees in Holland have to undergo rigorous physical tests and regular medical checks. In England the medical examination is left to the referee's own doctor and is only compulsory for FIFA referees. It is never searching enough. There have been several instances in recent years of referees dropping down dead while doing matches.

One of the good ideas introduced by the Football League is the bonus incentive scheme – £50 for referees in the top third, £37.50 in the middle and £25 for those nearer the bottom. The amounts have now been increased. But the referee is never told his marks. One referee receiving the £37.50 might be a mark or two off qualifying for the lowest grade. He might need to improve his performance to stay well up the next season. If he knew his markings he could do something about it. I can see nothing wrong with releasing the markings to the referees.

The League have cut down the amount of time it takes for a younger referee to get into the middle category after joining the League list, but it is still taking far too long for referees to get from the bottom to the top of the ladder. A lot of good referees are lost to the professional game because of this interminable qualification period which can take anything up to twelve or fourteen years. The best years of a referee's life are over by the time some of them are admitted to the League list.

I know several referees in minor football who have the ability and control to be successful in the Football League, but they have no chance of getting there. This is wrong. The County Associations know where the best material is and should pick out the top men and promote them over the heads of others.

Once having reached the supplementary list it is now possible for a referee to get on the full list inside a couple of years. But far too few referees are picked out from junior football at the right time. They have to wait along with all the others.

Bobby Charlton has said he thinks referees have become too important in the professional game and are getting too much publicity. I think he is right. This is something else the older referee never had to live with. Today's referee is analysed on TV and becomes known to millions of people.

There is nothing the referee can do about this. He cannot refuse to be photographed. Referees don't intentionally make themselves important. It is thrust upon them. Most referees would far prefer not to be noticed.

I feel, however, that the image of the referee could be bettered if the occasional referee was allowed to be interviewed on TV. In my last year I was turned down five times by the League when I sought permission to appear on TV. The public sees the actions of the referee on TV and hears these actions being criticized but the referee has no opportunity to present his side of the story.

Bobby Charlton also said that he felt some referees blew up for an offence without being certain in their minds which side should be penalized. 'They allow themselves to be influenced by what the players say,' he said. I do not think this is true. Certainly not in my experience. Every referee has his opinion about which way the free kick should be given, rightly or wrongly. Very few referees have ever allowed their judgement to be affected by what players say. If they do, they are not fit to be on the League list.

Positioning is the key. If the referee is close to the incident, he knows himself what has happened. But how often does he hear a shout from a player forty or fifty yeards away? How many times do strikers shout for offside in the other half of the field?

There may be plenty of advice coming from the players, but no referee acts on it. This is something which Bobby Charlton and his fellow players could do something about themselves. If there was less appealing, less chat, the modern game would be played in a far better spirit. But how often do we find the referee being blamed for incidents which in fact have been started by comments made by players? Far too often, I am afraid.

Managers have a clear responsibility. They should tell their players to respect the decisions of the referee and get on with the game. I feel they should have a code of conduct for their players pinned up in the dressing-room. If a player infringes it, he should be fined.

Very few managers take disciplinary action for such things as dissent, time-wasting, conning the referee, tackling unfairly; yet they have the power to impose fines and often do so for other offences such as arriving late for training or staying out late at night.

Would former players make better referees? I think perhaps they could, provided they were good referees, had control and didn't make mistakes. But if Bobby Charlton, for instance, took up refereeing he would only retain his immense reputation until the moment he made his first mistake or cautioned his first player. He would soon be disliked then.

Players would say the same things to him that they said to me, like 'You're taking my living away'. And, most amazing of the lot, 'I've got a wife and four kids to support.'

I remember Eddie Colquhoun, the Sheffield United and Scottish centre-half, saying to me in one match, 'You're giving us nothing, ref.' What did he expect me to be, Father Christmas? Did he think I was out there to 'give' things to either side instead of trying to arbitrate fairly?

I think there are many players today who would make good referees, particularly the nicer, more responsible type of player like Charlton himself. A point which is often overlooked is that nearly all the referees on the League list have played football themselves, if only at a low level, so they do know something about it. An over-the-top tackle in a junior game at the park is the same as the over-the-top tackle at Villa Park.

The complaint of many players is that referees are taking physical contact out of the game, but I do not believe this. In fact, I would say there was more physical contact in my last year as a League referee than in my first year. There were certainly more unpleasantness, more niggle and more professional fouls.

There will always be fouling and players getting hurt, even if the match were between two teams of angels. Referees have no desire to see the English game become like the Continental and South American game, where there is more emphasis on intercepting the ball and less on dispossessing opponents by the straight-forward tackle. They believe that fair tackling is part of the game and have no desire to see it eliminated.

What may appear to be a foul in the eyes of one referee may look unintentional to another referee. This is why there will always be inconsistency. It simply isn't possible to get eighty-odd people thinking the same way about everything. But a lot of work has gone into the training of referees in this country, and there is more uniformity today in regard to positioning and signals than ever before. The Association of Football League Referees and Linesmen is always seeking ways of improving standards.

Should there be more contact between the players and the referees? I think so. But the clubs don't seem to want it. No club will refuse a referee permission to train on its premises, but they never press the point.

More contact would remedy many of the things which are wrong in player-referee relationships. The players say we don't know the game. Are they all so highly intelligent and the referees all so ignorant? Don't we know the difference between 4-4-2 and 4-2-4? Are we not supposed to know what a blind-side run is? Or be able to recognize a bad pass? There are a high number of referees who are qualified FA coaches, so they must know something about the game. Just the same as there are a few players who are qualified referees.

Some critics have suggested that there should be electronic aids to judge when a ball has crossed the line, and the like. I can see no place for these devices in the game. Football is about people, not computers and machines. It is about people and what they think.

Football is so popular because it is an outlet. People argue about whether the ball went over the line, and whether the referee was right. If a computer came up with the right answer every time there would be nothing to argue about and the game would die.

One aspect where there is room for improvement is the treating of referees' injuries. The local professional club will usually treat an injured referee, but as the referee cannot get there until the evening, that is not much help.

Mostly, I paid for my own treatment. But I think the League could launch its own fund to pay for the treatment of referees. There is, however, an insurance scheme run by the League which pays out to referees who are off work through injury.

I refereed my first game on the Beaconsfield just off the Great Yarmouth prom twenty years ago. I was very nervous and when I got out to the middle, I thought to myself: 'What the hell am I doing out here?'

When the game got started, one of the players went down injured. I didn't think it was very serious so I allowed play to continue. The other players stopped playing on their own accord to enable the injured player to be treated.

Now, twenty years later, I wonder what would happen if I made the same error of judgement in a Football League game? Would the players stop? Or would they carry on and try and gain some advantage? In too many clubs they would carry on.

That, to me, is the predicament which the professional game has got itself into. As football has become more a business and less a sport, the spirit of the game which has evolved since the early days has almost disappeared. That is the sad part.

I enjoyed my twenty years, especially the last eleven on the League list. People ask me what I got out of it, as there was little money. Something you can't define in real terms – a sense of being involved in a game you love.

For me, it was enough to have taken part. When people ask me what I am to do now, I don't know the answer. All I know is that I shall miss football more than I can say.

Appendix 1

The Football League memorandum

The Football League Memorandum sent out on 16 August 1971 which launched the stricter interpretation of the laws of the game, or the referees' clampdown, was as follows:

OFFSIDE

(a) Referees must be satisfied that a player who is in an offside position *is interfering with play or seeking to gain an advantage* before he penalizes him for being offside.

(b) Linesmen should not 'flag' automatically if a player is in an offside position. Before indicating to the referee that a player is offside the linesman should ensure that the player is interfering with play or seeking to gain an advantage and should only 'flag' when he is satisfied that this is so.

(c) Having decided that a player is, in fact, offside, the referee should blow his whistle immediately and not await the result of the pass. If, however, the ball touches, or is played by an opponent, whilst he is going to blow his whistle (but has not already done so), he should not blow it. (The action of the ball touching or being played by an opposing player brings into effect the 'unless' clause, and referees are not entitled to ignore it.)

(d) Referees shall acknowledge *all* signals from linesmen. The acknowledgement may, of course, in some cases, take the form of penalizing a player.

OFFENCES AGAINST THE GOALKEEPPER. Referees must penalize the following:

(a) Jumping at the goalkeeper under the pretence of heading the ball. Punishable by a *direct* free kick.

(b) Raising the foot as the goalkeeper kicks the ball from his hands, even though the ball may have left the goalkeeper's hand. The above offence constitutes dangerous play and an indirect free kick should be awarded.

It was considered that no action could be taken against a player who stands in front of the goalkeeper to prevent him clearing the ball, or who moves from side to side with the goalkeeper. It is the responsibility of the goalkeeper to clear the ball even if only by throwing the ball. If, however, the player takes any action which could cause trouble or constitute obstruction the referee has discretionary power to take appropriate action.

FREE KICKS

(a) When raising the arm to indicate indirect free kicks the referee shall retain it in position until the ball has been played by a second player or goes out of play. This need not apply to offside indirect free kicks.

(b) In many cases referees are not implementing the caution when players fail to retire the correct distance or when they encroach at the taking of a free kick. This part of the law must be strictly enforced and referees should not leave players in any doubt that they intend to enforce it.

(c) Referees should no longer pace out the requisite ten yards at the taking of free kicks. It is considered that it is more dignified to stand at the point from where the free kick is to be taken and *ensure* that the opposing players retreat to the ten-yard position.

Referees to be advised of the urgent necessity for taking strong action to eliminate encroachment at the taking of free kicks.

ATTITUDE TOWARDS REFEREES AND LINESMEN

Protests (by word or action) against referees' decisions will result in a caution. Any player who molests a referee or linesman will be sent from the field.

TIME WASTING

Deliberate acts of time wasting must be penalized in accordance with the laws. Insofar as the last two sections are concerned there is a view that referees are failing to use their discretion sufficiently and are penalizing when it is debatable whether the players' action constituted an offence of dissent or *deliberate* time wasting.

DELIBERATE HANDLING OR CATCHING THE BALL

If a player deliberately catches or handles the ball to prevent an opponent gaining an advantage which, in the referee's opinion, would reasonably have occurred in the normal pattern of play, then the referee shall deem it to be ungentlemanly conduct.

And in addition to the direct free kick (or penalty) which he shall award for the offence of handling the ball, he shall caution the offending player.

DELIBERATE OBSTRUCTION

If a player deliberately interposes his body to prevent an opponent gaining an advantage which, in the referee's opinion, would reasonably have ocurred in the normal pattern of play, then the referee should deem it to be ungentlemanly conduct and he shall caution the offending player in addition to awarding the free kick.

DELIBERATE TRIPPING

If a player deliberately trips an opponent to prevent him gaining an advantage which, in the referee's opinion, would reasonably have occurred in the normal pattern of play, then the referee shall deem it to be ungentlemanly conduct and in addition to the direct free kick (or penalty) which he shall award for the offence of tripping, he will caution the offending player.

The above three offences are examples of what are being termed 'professional fouls'.

TACKLING

For some time the emphasis seems to have been to caution players for technical offences (showing dissent, time wasting, etc) but to ignore the necessity to caution for more serious or dangerous offences. Many referees are failing to take action when offences of the following nature are committed:

(a) With foot lifted from the ground. This is permissible unless it is seen to be dangerous to the opponent.

(b) With both feet together. Also permissible unless seen to be dangerous to the opponent.

(c) Sliding tackle, with one or both legs. This is permissible, but if the ball is not played and the opponent is tripped, the punishment will be a direct free kick.

Where any of the above offences occur, the referee may caution the player in addition to awarding a free kick.

(d) tackle from behind – (i) through a player's legs. (ii) round a player.

If the ball is played without the player first touching an opponent's legs, this is allowed. If the opponent's legs are touched first a direct free kick will be awarded. If the opponent is first charged from behind (unless he is unintentionally obstructed) a direct free kick will be awarded. If there is no clear indication to play the ball, a direct free kick will be awarded if the player is tripped. (Note: It is suggested that it is almost impossible to tackle fairly from behind *through a player's legs*.)

For this offence (d), a referee shall caution the player in addition to awarding the free kick.

DIAGONAL SYSTEM OF CONTROL

Referees are adhering too rigidly to the 'true diagonal' and should be instructed to adjust their method of control in accordance with the requirements of the game.

A strong view was expressed that para 15 of 'Appendix B, Standing Orders Relating to Referees and Linesmen' should be amended to give referees more discretion in the most advantageous use of linesmen.

The diagonal system will continue to be the basic method of control but within this system the referees may use the linesmen in the most appropriate manner.

CONTROL

The League's main interest is that the referees should *control* the players. How they do this is their own concern as long as they do it.

The League does not intend to interfere with the method of refereeing, but the purpose of these meetings is to give guidance on the things on which the League requires certain action to be taken. These matters have the full approval of the FA, as does the action which is required to be taken.

Reproduced by permission of the Football League.

Appendix 2

The new code of disciplinary procedures, 1972-73

1 REPORTING OF OFFENCES

(a) Caution offences

(i) Referees will continue to administer field cautions in accordance with the laws of the game.

(ii) Referees and linesmen must submit a report in duplicate containing details of the offence to the FA within two days of the match.

(iii) A copy of the referee's report and, where appropriate, copies of the linesmens' reports will be forwarded by the FA to the player, who will be advised of the number of penalty points recorded against him for the offence.

(b) Sending off offences

(i) Referees and linesmen must submit a report in duplicate containing details of the offence to the FA within two days of the match.

(ii) Copies of the referee's and linesmens' reports will be forwarded to the player accompanied by a letter advising him that the offence is one for which he will automatically be subject to disciplinary action (see section 4).

2 PERSONAL HEARINGS

(a) Four point penalty offence. On receiving notification that a four point penalty offence has been recorded against him, a player shall be entitled to:

182

(i) apply to the FA for a personal hearing to rebut the charge set out in the referee's report provided such application is received by the FA within ten days of the match and is accompanied by the player's version of the incident, or

(ii) give notice to the FA that in the event of his accumlating twelve or more penalty points prior to the end of the season he may wish to contest the recording of the offence at a personal hearing. When giving such notice to the FA, the player must submit his version of the relevant incident.

(b) 1, 2 and 3 point penalty offence. On receiving notification that a 1, 2 or 3 point penalty offence has been recorded against him, a player may give notice that he may wish to contest the recording of the offence in the event of his accumulating twelve or more penalty points during the season and thereby be liable to disciplinary action. Such notice must be lodged with the FA within ten days of the match and must be accompanied by the player's version of the incident. At this time the FA will then make available to the player and to the referee and linesmen copies of all relevant reports and statements.

Members of the Disciplinary Committee will be appointed to deal with personal hearings as and when necessary. A player who has requested a personal hearing will be advised under the provisions of FA rule 39 of the time, date and place of the hearing. A player requesting a personal hearing may be required to pay Commission costs incurred not exceeding £50 in the event of the case being found proved.

Three members of the Disciplinary Committee will be appointed to each Commission unless the Chairman of the Disciplinary Committee shall decide otherwise.

In the event of a Commission consisting of more than three members the Commission costs to be met by a player will be restricted to the expenses of three of the members only, plus administrative costs.

Once a player has lodged an application for a personal hearing with the FA he will not be permitted to withdraw such application except *in exceptional circumstances and only* with the permission of the Council which will not readily be given.

3 PLAYERS ACCUMULATING 12 PENALTY POINTS WITHIN A SEASON
When a player has accumulated a total of twelve or more penalty points during a season he will be subject automatically to the agreed standard punishment for twelve penalty points namely a two-match suspension (see Section 5) unless he wishes to exercise the options concerning personal hearings as laid down in Section 2. A player who applies for a personal hearing under the provisions of Section 2 (b) must indicate the particular charge(s) he wishes to challenge.

4 PLAYERS SENT OFF
A player who is sent off the field of play will be provided with copies of the referee's and linesmens' reports together with a covering letter advising him that he will be subject to the agreed standard punishment, namely a three-match suspension (see Section 5) unless he wishes to contest the charge contained in the referee's report, in which case he must, within ten days of the date of the match, lodge with the FA an application for a personal hearing.

5 STANDARD PUNISHMENTS
(a) Subject to a player's right to a personal hearing as defined in Sections 2 and 4, the following standard punishments will operate automatically:
(i) Sending off offences – a player will be suspended from all matches (private training sessions between players of the same club excepted) commencing ten days from the date of the match in which the offence occurred and until such time as the club's recognized senior team has *completed* three matches in approved competitions during the period covered by its opening match in the Football League competition and ending with the final match in which the club is playing in a domestic competition organized by the FA or Football League.
(ii) Caution offences totalling twelve points – the player will be suspended from all matches until such time as the club's recognized senior team has competed the recognized competion matches as outlined in (i) above. The suspension will commence ten days after the date of the match in which the player received his final offence.

(b) Fines will not be imposed on players for field offences. Clubs must not pay a player more than his basic wage during the period of suspension.

(c) The penalties outlined in a (i) and a (ii) above will apply automatically.

(d) Any penalty of match suspension which remains outstanding at the end of a season must be served at the commencement of the next season.

6 INDEPENDENT APPEALS TRIBUNAL

(a) A player will have the right of appeal to an Independent Appeals Tribunal against punishment:

(i) imposed for a sending-off offence which incurs a three-match penalty.

(ii) imposed as a result of accumulating twelve penalty points for offences at least two of which carry a four point penalty.

(b) The Appeals Tribunal will comprise an independent chairman, a nominee of the FA and a nominee of the PFA.

(c) The provisions of Rule 39 (b) relating to representation at a personal hearing will apply to appeals made to the Tribunal.

(d) In any unsuccessful appeal to the Tribunal the player requesting the Appeal may be liable to costs not exceeding £50.

7 PENALTY POINTS FOR CAUTIONS

(a) The following scale of points for caution offences will be applicable until further notice:

Law 1	Illegal marking of the pitch	1
Law 12	Deliberate handling of the ball	2
„	obstruction	3
„	tripping	4
	Entering or re-entering the field without referee's permission	1
	Persistent infringement of the laws	3
	Showing dissent, including	
	(a) interference by other players when referee is speaking to player(s) after an offence	

(b) continued commenting to referee concerning his decisions in an effort to intimidate him   4

Wasting time   2

Shirt pulling etc   3

Goalkeeper wasting time (section 5b)   2

Player using shoulders of his own team colleague to assist him in heading ball   1

Moving arms about to obstruct opponent   2

Goalkeeper lying on ball to waste time   2

Dangerous play   4

Foul tackle from behind   4

Law 13   Encroachment within ten yards of ball   3

Gesticulating in front of player taking the kick   2

Law 14   Encroachment by a defender   2

Encroachment by an attacker   2

Gesticulating by kicker   2

Law 15   Gesticulating in front of thrower   2

Any other offence deemed by the referee to be ungentlemanly conduct under the discretionary powers granted to him by Law 5   2

(b) In the event of a player's offences totalling more than twelve points, the points in excess of twelve will be carried forward and added to any further points he may receive during the same season.